Hiking Michigan

Help Us Keep This Guide Up to Date

Every effort has been made by the author and editors to make this guide as accurate and useful as possible. However, many things can change after a guide is published—trails are rerouted, regulations change, techniques evolve, facilities come under new management, etc.

We would love to hear from you concerning your experiences with this guide and how you feel it could be improved and kept up to date. While we may not be able to respond to all comments and suggestions, we'll take them to heart and we'll also make certain to share them with the author. Please send your comments and suggestions to the following address:

The Globe Pequot Press
Reader Response/Editorial Department
P.O. Box 480
Guilford, CT 06437

Or you may e-mail us at:

editorial@GlobePequot.com

Thanks for your input, and happy travels!

Hiking
Michigan

Second Edition

Mike Modrzynski

FALCON®

GUILFORD, CONNECTICUT
HELENA, MONTANA
AN IMPRINT OF THE GLOBE PEQUOT PRESS

A FALCON GUIDE®

All photos by the author.

ISSN 1544-4570
ISBN 0-7627-2700-4

Manufactured in the United States of America
Second Edition/First Printing

Contents

Weekend Hikes

Nature Hikes

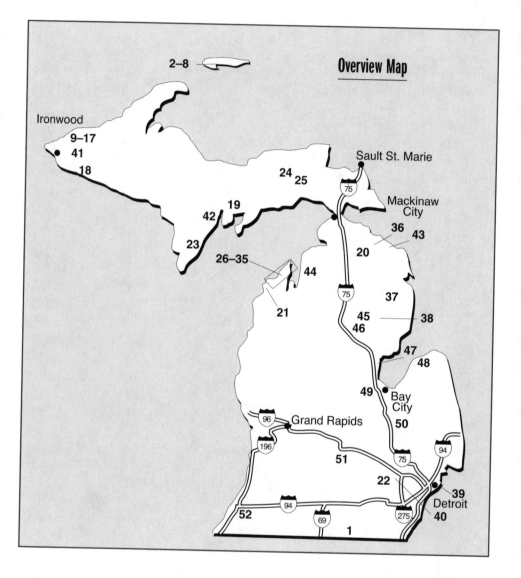

Overview Map

2–8

Ironwood

9–17
41
18

24 25

Sault St. Marie

75

Mackinaw
City

36 43

19

42

23

26–35

44

20

75

37

21

45
46

38

47

48

49

Bay
City

50

96

Grand Rapids

196

51

75

94

22

39
Detroit

40

52

94

69

275

1

Introduction

Michigan's many trails run the gamut from urban walks to total wilderness treks. Spreading across two peninsulas, they afford hikers the chance to explore the mixed history of the patchwork quilt called "The Wolverine State" in a day, a weekend, or an entire summer. Hundreds of trails lace the Michigan countryside, providing hiking opportunities along sandy or cliff shores of four of the five Great Lakes, in the region's northern mountains, or in its vast forests.

Hikers who have a spirit of adventure and a taste for wilderness will find trails in the state's Upper Peninsula to their liking-especially those in the Porcupine Mountains or on stark and beautiful Isle Royale, alone in Lake Superior. The Lower Peninsula provides its own brand of accessible wilderness, the crowning jewel of which is the High Country Pathway through Pigeon River State Forest in the northern half of lower Michigan's "mitten." And for those with a summer to while away, there is always the state's 875-mile stretch of the national North Country Trail, which guides hikers across Michigan's full spectrum.

Trail users in Michigan also benefit from a union with the state Department of Natural Resources (DNR), which has helped preserve and extend the web of trails in the state through its Rails-to-Trails Program. The rail trails and other Michigan routes meander through historic lumber camps long ago reclaimed by forest, go across giant tracts of wetlands and their fragile ecosystems, and head into the heart of wilderness. Stand on the ridges of Isle Royale and wonder at the insignificance of human life in the midst of Lake Superior's power and beauty. Marvel at the breathtaking view from the overlook above Lake of the Clouds in the Porcupine Mountains. These experiences and more are found along the thousands of trail miles that Michigan offers.

This book is by no means a complete inventory of Michigan's hiking trails, but it does look at each of the state's regions and opens doors in each area. One person could spend a lifetime hiking the hundreds of available trails and, given the DNR's commitment to opening new routes, the task would be never-ending. Hikers who want to begin somewhere can take this guide in hand, take stock of their abilities and interests, then plan a hike in Michigan. The opportunities are endless.

Using This Guidebook

Some wilderness hikes in both the Upper and Lower Peninsulas may require either time or a level of conditioning not within the grasp of the average hiker, but most trails can be handled by even the casual trekker. Most trails in Michigan require more determination than skill—more grit than guts—to complete. But don't ever underestimate the hazards of careless hiking. Plan ahead, and know your limitations.

The unmatched beauty of a sunrise over the islands and watery channels surrounding Isle Royale National Park.

The hikes described in this book are organized into three sections based on hikers' time limitations, not trail difficulty. The **extended hikes** described in the first section are just that—longer hikes that will require extended stays in the backcountry. These routes demand reliance on camping and other outdoor skills. **Weekend hikes** are, in many cases, just shorter versions of an extended hike and often call on many of the same skills and same degree of knowledge. Nature hikes offer short routes for families and inexperienced hikers who nevertheless want to enjoy the outdoors.

The main intent of this guide is to provide information that helps hikers choose trails that match their desires and abilities. Each entry provides a detailed description of a trail and notes its natural and historic features. Each trail description begins with an outline of the physical characteristics of the trail, for quick and easy reference.

A general description comes first. This brief description is followed by notes on trail difficulty, which can be interpreted as follows: **Easy** trails are relatively short, flat, and well marked and can be completed without difficulty by hikers of all abilities; **moderate** trails will challenge novices with steeper grades or navigational requirements; **difficult** routes will tax experienced hikers in grades, route-finding, and/or length.

Entries also list suggested maps and give the address for the managing agency (or agencies), compiled in Appendix B. Use this guide in partnership with local area maps, topographic quads, and other resources, such as those listed. Be prepared to use a compass and map on strenuous hikes, extended hikes, and many wilderness hikes.

After the initial reference notes, each hike entry features a mile-by-mile description of landmarks, trail junctions, and environments. This section tells hikers what to expect along the trail and also offers tips on safety, common weather occurrences, wildlife, and more. The maps and photographs in this book may also help you get a feel for the trails before you hike them. A few chapters in this book include **Honorable Mentions**—additional trails and hikes that you may wish to explore.

Camping on State and Federal Lands

Camping along many of the trails in Michigan is restricted to designated campgrounds, but on many of the more remote systems, on both state and federal lands, hikers have some freedom in selecting a spot to pitch a tent. A few restrictions, however, may apply; these are designed to preserve the environment along the trails and to maintain the rustic nature of such trails as the North Country Trail and the High Country Pathway.

Several areas have specific regulations regarding camping. For instance, the Sylvania Wilderness, a hidden gem of the Upper Peninsula, allows camping only in developed locations around each of its lakes. Camping is allowed in designated sites under USDA Forest Service regulations that restrict the number of campers and regulate campfires, cooking, and firewood gathering.

Ravines carved by feeder creeks are spanned by wooden footbridges in the Herman Vogler Conservation Area.

In most state and federal forests, the rules are more lenient, permitting hikers to select their own campsites with only a few restrictions as to where they might be placed. Campsites must be at least 200 feet from lakes, streams, and/or wetlands; construction of any sort of permanent structure is prohibited, including a toilet facility. Soapy water must be disposed of at least 200 feet from any water source, and bathing in streams or lakes is prohibited.

For detailed information, contact:
Michigan Department of Natural Resources
Forest Management Division
P.O. Box 30452
Lansing, Michigan 48909-7952

Michigan Department of Natural Resources
Parks and Recreation Division
P.O. Box 30028
Lansing, Michigan 48909

Hikers may also want to write or call the specific references for each area, as mentioned in the "For More Information" section of each hike entry or listed in Appendix B.

Clothing and Equipment

Hikers who are unused to Michigan's variable weather should plan for all types of climate. Dress warmly, in waterproof and wicking layers, especially in wilderness areas such as the Porcupine Mountains or Isle Royale. Lakeshore weather and wilderness experiences require that visitors plan for the probability of cool, damp evenings.

Hypothermia, the dangerous lowering of the body's core temperature, is not usually considered a danger during the milder hiking seasons in Michigan. But it is a real problem year-round and can happen without the usual accompaniment of bone-chilling temperatures. Hikers can become hypothermic in temperatures just below 50 degrees Fahrenheit, if conditions are right. Particularly in spring and fall, hypothermia can arrive dramatically; before you know it, you can be well on your way to trouble.

Be aware that conditions that can create hypothermia exist throughout the year. Avoid chilling sweat by planning ahead and pacing yourself to avoid overexertion. During a hike, stop as often as necessary to catch up with the effects weather or hard work is having on your body, and carry extra rain gear and clothing to replace damp or sweat-soaked garb.

Water: Is It Safe?

Water is one item hikers will find in great amounts in Michigan, but none of it should be considered safe enough to drink as found. As pure as the brooks and streams of wilderness areas may seem, do not attempt to drink from them without first boiling or filtering the water.

Streams, brooks, and springs are all home to a large number of bacteria, protozoa, and viruses. In Michigan the most notable, and potentially hazardous, is the protozoan *Giardia lamblia,* an intestinal parasite that has spoiled more hikes than anything except, maybe, the weather. *Giardia* thrives in cold, clear streams and lakes and is carried in the intestines and feces of beaver, muskrat, moose, and other animals that live or feed in lakes and streams.

Wildlife

One of the benefits of hiking in Michigan is the chance to observe its wildlife. The state is home to more than 200 species of songbirds, plus one of the largest herds of white-tailed deer in the United States and the largest free-roaming herd of elk east of the Mississippi River. Hikers may see coyotes, foxes, raccoons, wild turkeys, rabbits, and other small game.

The state also is home to two major predators, the wolf and the black bear. Gray wolves in Michigan's Upper Peninsula, once common only on Lake Superior's

The birdlife along the Bay de Noc–Grand Island Trail is diverse and includes many raptors, including the great horned owl.

Isle Royale, now are found in all the Upper Peninsula's counties. The population has grown to nearly 300 animals. Michigan Department of Natural Resources wildlife biologist Jim Hammill says that the gray wolf has returned to claim its rightful place in the state's wildlife ecosystem.

According to Hammill, the Upper Peninsula environment, vast areas of uninhabited wilderness, and bountiful prey animals have made the return of the gray wolf one of the state's proudest wildlife success stories. Although the wolves are not concentrated in any one county, there are probably more of the animals in the central and northern counties. In the area around St. Ignace (Mackinac County), there are at least three packs with four to six animals in each family group. There are known wolf packs near other populated areas of the Upper Peninsula, but most wolves are reclusive and inhabit backcountry areas favored by their prey.

Although the chance of encountering a wolf is a rare and those meetings will be brief, the presence of these large canines should be factored into any hike through Michigan's Upper Peninsula. Although not generally people-friendly, wolves are not shy about investigating a poorly maintained campsite, open food, or people in their backyards.

Black bears are found in nearly every county in the state. Hikers must take precautions to avoid confrontations with either wolves or bears, especially when camping or transporting food.

Face-to-face encounters with either predator are unlikely, but both wolves and bears are attracted to food sources, including garbage. They may also be met on the trail; hikers should avoid travel routes favored by bears (look for scat as a warning) and should hike during the day, when bears are least active. A few more tips for hiking in bear and wolf country:

- Stay on established trails, and make noise while traveling.
- Avoid hiking during the early morning and late evening.
- Don't camp in an area obviously frequented by bears or wolves. If you see a bear or a wolf or fresh sign where you intend to camp, pick another site.
- Set up your tent or sleeping area away from cooking areas.
- Keep a clean camp, and avoid food odors. Lock food in a vehicle or suspend it from a nearby tree. Double-bag garbage to avoid attracting uninvited guests.
- Do not camp near game trails.
- If possible, camp near trees that can be climbed if a bear pursues you (a highly unlikely event with a wolf). You can't outrun a bear, so don't plan to. Although black bears do climb trees, some defense is better than no defense.

Our wild state is also home to a variety of smaller, flying critters that cause human discomfort. There never seems to be a time—except for frozen winter—when there isn't some kind of bug around to cause problems. In early spring, wet areas are the natural breeding grounds for many of the worst winged pests. Once the hordes of blackflies disappear in mid-June, mosquitos arrive on the scene. And, of course, there is the ever-present tick to keep things interesting.

Using repellents can be the most effective preventive measure, but be sure to use appropriate ones that meet your specific needs. To avoid compounding medical problems or risking your health, be aware of the effects and contents of the repellents you use. Using DEET or permethrin on clothing and a lotion repellent on your skin builds a most effective anti-insect system.

Following are some basic guidelines for avoiding most bugs:

- Spray clothing and other gear with permethrin before you leave for your hike.
- Use lotions, sprays, or creams on exposed skin.
- Use specific repellents for specific bugs. Not all repellents work on all species. Citronella works against mosquitos, for instance, but is useless against black-flies.
- Keep in mind that strong chemical repellents may be irritants and in some cases could endanger your health. Use them sparingly and wisely.

Besides wolves, bears, and insects, Michigan hikers have one other living trail hazard: the Massasauga rattlesnake, or swamp rattler, the state's only poisonous snake. Massasauga rattlers are small, mild-mannered snakes found in wet and low-lying areas. They are dark, spotted, and hard to spot in the undergrowth. Rarely seen outside a swamp environment, these small snakes are prevalent throughout the state but most common in the northeastern Lower Peninsula.

Zero Impact

Conscientious hikers don't need the reminder, and others probably won't read it, but here it is nevertheless: Garbage does not change its character in a wilderness setting. The motto "Pack It In, Pack It Out" is the golden rule of responsible hiking. Remember that glass, aluminum foil, and disposable juice containers are not meant for burning in backcountry campfires and that cigarette butts and candy wrappers never seem to disappear. Our obligation to respect and protect the trailside environment means that we all must do our part to ensure that the terrain we travel retains no record of our passing. To keep wilderness beautiful and remote, and to maintain our trails as a natural experience, please be aware of your impact on the land. Walk lightly, and leave no trace.

Michigan offers a lifetime of hiking opportunities, with trails stretching from shore to shore and along the length and width of two peninsulas. To make sure this treasure remains for future generations, take only pictures and memories.

◀ *Although black bears are rarely seen, hikers need to stay aware of their presence.*

Trailside raspberries on the Shore-to-Shore Trail.

Michigan's Rails-to-Trails Program

Michigan's extensive railroad system once linked logging operations, mines, and far-flung agricultural regions with the state's sprawling industrialized areas. In this century, many of these train tracks lapsed into disrepair, pushed into obscurity by reduced markets and a modern highway system. Today many of these weed-choked lines with rotting ties and rusting rails have found new life as part of Michigan's Rails-to-Trails Program.

The Michigan Trailways Act, passed by the Michigan Legislature in 1993, authorized and encouraged creation of a trailway system along the state's 5,000 miles of unused rail lines. Local governments, organizations, private citizens, and the Department of Natural Resources (DNR) have worked together to create this multiagency, multiuse trail network. Since 1970 the DNR and other agencies have reclaimed nearly 750 miles of the nearly 10,000 miles of tracks that once spread like a spider's web across both peninsulas. The program originally was intended to create snowmobile trails but has benefited hikers, mountain bikers, and equestrians as well. In time, state officials hope to double the number of available miles.

The rail trails are ideal for many uses. Their gentle grade changes and extended flat runs appeal to planners trying to include less-active or physically impaired hikers, as well as snowmobilers and bikers. They link diverse environments, passing through urban, rural, and even semiwilderness settings. Where the trails pass deserted lumbering and mining towns, they are living historical pathways as well, providing educational opportunities along with recreation. In more remote areas, they open access to some of the state's out-of-the-way rivers and lakes and are a means of reaching a natural laboratory of plants and wildlife otherwise undisturbed by the mechanized world.

Because they link several regions of the state, the rails-to-trails systems can help hikers create more accessible routes. Backcountry users can follow the lines to transform a closed-loop hike into a weeklong trek across Michigan. The DNR's hope is to eventually link most major trails so that trail users can begin outings at any number of points in an easy, convenient way.

DNR personnel have already acquired a large number of rail corridors or segments as parts of the spreading snowmobile trail system that covers much of northern Michigan. This has been a three-season bounty for hikers and other nonmechanized users. The fifteen "snowmobile" routes amount to nearly 300 miles of public trails in dry seasons. These are mainly located in the Upper Peninsula but include one 23-mile segment linking Mackinaw City to Alanson in the Lower Peninsula.

Other Rails-to-Trails sections include:

- **Hart-Montague Trail** winds for 21 miles across portions of Oceana and Muskegon Counties in western Michigan. The property was donated to the state by a private citizen and in 1988 was designated Hart-Montague State Park. The entire length of the trail has recently been paved to open it to more users.

- **Kal-Haven Trail and Sesquicentennial State Park,** another reclaimed rail corridor, links metropolitan Kalamazoo and South Haven in southwestern Michigan. This 38-mile paved trail is open to all modes of nonmechanized travel spring through fall and is open to snowmobiles once there is sufficient snow cover. The public Friends of the Kal-Haven Trail group is a strong force behind the improvement and care of this right-of-way.
- **Paint Creek Trail** offers access to one of southern Michigan's finest blue-ribbon trout fisheries and is free of the antagonizing din of motorized pests. The 8.5-mile trail isn't paved but has been improved with a gravel cap that makes hiking easy, even for anglers in waders. The trail links Lake Orion and Rochester, providing a quiet getaway near an urban setting. A 0.5-mile stretch of right-of-way purchased by the DNR connects this placid trail to the Rochester-Utica Recreation Area.
- **Lakelands Trail State Park,** a 31-mile stretch of pathway, links the communities of Jackson and Hamburg in southern Michigan
- **The South Lyon to Wixom** right-of-way is a 7-mile corridor in western Oakland County that DNR officials hope eventually to link to the Lakelands system.
- **Bay City to Pinconning** right-of-ways contain two short segments of abandoned railbed. The first is a 3.7-mile segment located next to the Nayanquing Point Wildlife Area and is currently managed by the DNR Wildlife Division. The other, shorter segment is a 2-mile stretch connecting Bay City State Park with Tobico Marsh State Game Area.

In Oakland County, a 4-mile stretch of rail line in West Bloomfield Township will eventually be joined to other nonmechanized trails in the region. Midland County now owns a right-of-way that will eventually link Midland to Clare.

Since 1992 the DNR has added three other major abandoned rail segments to the rails-to-trails inventory. Over the next few years the DNR, in partnership with communities throughout Michigan, hopes to develop a total 1,311 miles to be included in the program. The longest segment, the Grand Rapids to Cadillac Line, or "White Pine Trail," as it is known locally, goes for 90 miles through diverse ecosystems. The east-west Clare to Baldwin line adds another 50 miles to the inventory.

Brief but vital to the program in southwest Michigan are the 16 miles of rail grade from South Haven to Hartford. This short segment will become part of the Kal-Haven Trail. It runs through farmland and forest and is quite remote. The Parks and Recreation Division will manage the trail as a unit of Van Buren State Park, 2 miles away, which may someday be linked to the path by a trail spur.

Approval has also been given to purchase two short segments of rail corridor in Pellston and Brutus in Emmet County, to bridge gaps in the 23-mile trail connecting Mackinaw City to Alanson. The DNR plans to develop the complete corridor as a multiuse trail system and, eventually, extend it into Petoskey.

Thus far, there are more than 225 miles of completed or designated railbed trails in Michigan's Lower Peninsula. The DNR has proposed adding another 500 miles of abandoned rail corridor to the inventory. The department already owns 300 miles of abandoned right-of-way in the Upper Peninsula, used primarily by snowmobilers.

Michigan rail line right-of-ways are being abandoned at a rate of more than 100 miles each year. These segments are being incorporated into state or local recreation areas as they become available, contributing to the state's Rails-to-Trails Program. For more information on the program, contact:

Jim Radabaugh
Acting State Trails Coordinator
Forest Management Division
Michigan Department of Natural Resources
P.O. Box 30452
Lansing, Michigan 48909-7952
(517) 373–0367
E-mail: hagane@state.mi.us

Map Legend

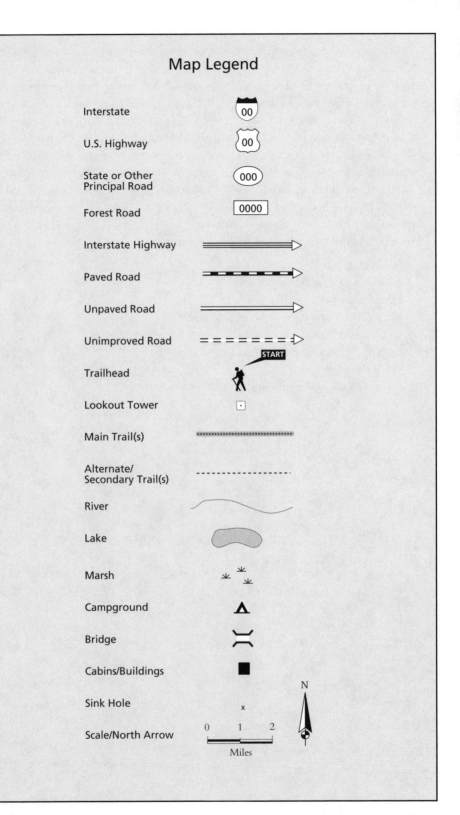

Interstate	
U.S. Highway	00
State or Other Principal Road	000
Forest Road	0000
Interstate Highway	
Paved Road	
Unpaved Road	
Unimproved Road	
Trailhead	START
Lookout Tower	
Main Trail(s)	
Alternate/ Secondary Trail(s)	
River	
Lake	
Marsh	
Campground	
Bridge	
Cabins/Buildings	
Sink Hole	x
Scale/North Arrow	N 0 1 2 Miles

Extended
Hikes

North Country Trail

S ince the North Country Scenic Trail (NCT) was first considered in 1980, more than 1,700 miles of the anticipated 4,500-mile trail system have been certified, and the amount of usable trail is approaching the 3,000-mile mark. Few hikers have hiked the entire distance from New York to North Dakota, but the trail remains an adventure, since many of the segments of the system require a bit of improvisation to navigate. Michigan's 875-mile segment of the NCT is the largest piece of the seven-state puzzle. The Wolverine State also contains the most certified miles, about 450, most in the Upper Peninsula and the northern third of the Lower Peninsula. Add to that nearly 125 miles of usable trail, and it's easy to see why long distance hikers enjoy Michigan's portion of this national trail system.

In Michigan the NCT passes through farmland, forests, urban sprawl, and even wilderness areas as it meanders north from the Ohio border, near the village of Waldron, to the city of Ironwood in the western Upper Peninsula and the gateway to Wisconsin's portion of the NCT. Trails pass through areas considered "a walk in the park" and suddenly enter stretches of forest or lakeshore that will challenge even veteran hikers. The links in Michigan's portion of the NCT enable hikers to plan a day hike or trek a week or more along the route.

Although the route avoids the heavily populated southeast corner of Michigan and is located nearly entirely along the western half of the Lower Peninsula, it provides hikers with a glimpse into every facet of the state's rich mixed heritage. Much of the trail meanders through rural farmland, parks, and backcountry roads and even traces abandoned railroad beds. Hikers will enter Michigan's vast forested area near White Cloud and the historic Birch Grove Schoolhouse, once the headquarters of the North Country Trail Association. From here it's rolling farmland, thick forests, river valleys, and the shoreline of northern Lake Michigan before reaching the Straits of Mackinac.

The Mackinac Bridge, the 5-mile-long suspension bridge connecting Michigan's two peninsulas, is the only obstacle hikers will find difficult to surmount, since walking the span is permitted only once a year, and then only north to south. Other highlights along the trail's course through the Upper Peninsula include Tahquamenon Falls, the second largest waterfall east of the Mississippi River, Pictured Rocks National Lakeshore, and Porcupine Mountains State Park.

1 North Country Trail

Highlights: The longest segment of the seven-state North Country Trail, offering a complete look at urban and rural Michigan.

Type of hike: Backpack linear hike.

Total distance: 875 miles.

Difficulty: Lower Peninsula, easy to moderate; Upper Peninsula, moderate to difficult.

Best months: Any, but snowy weather precludes hiking in the Upper Peninsula in winter.

Maps: Available from the North Country Trail Association, 49 Monroe Center, Suite 200B, Grand Rapids, MI 49503. Lower Peninsula—State Line to Calhoun County; Kalamazoo County to Kent County; Newaygo County to Wexford County; Grand Traverse County to Antrim County; Charlevoix County to Mackinaw City. Upper Peninsula—St. Ignace to Marquette; Marquette to Ironwood.

Permits and fees: $2.50 each way to cross the Mackinac Bridge by private vehicle; $2.00 for pedestrian shuttle.

Special considerations: The variety of terrain from county roads to mountains in the Upper Peninsula will require footwear to match the hike; lowland crossings will be wet in the spring.

For more information: North Country Trail Association, 49 Monroe Center, Suite 200B, Grand Rapids, MI 49503.

Parking and trailhead facilities: Since both trailheads are close to the communities marking the entrance and exit for Michigan's segment of the NCT, hikers will find all the necessary services to make the hike an enjoyable one.

Key points: The Mackinac Bridge, Mackinac Island, Tahquamenon Falls, Pictured Rocks National Lakeshore, the Porcupine Mountains.

Finding the trailhead: Literally hundreds of trailheads exist along the 875 miles of the NCT in Michigan, given the number of road crossings and trail links. The two main trailheads are near the village of Waldron along the Ohio-Michigan border and Ironwood in the western Upper Peninsula.

To find the Waldron trailhead, follow Lee Road south from the village of Waldron to the Ohio border. The border crossing is the unofficial trailhead.

To reach the Ironwood trailhead, take U.S. Highway 2 into Ironwood from Wisconsin. The on-road trailhead is on the highway bridge over the Montreal River.

The hike:

The hike described below tracks south to north and provides only a brief, general overview of the trail's segments. Hikers intending to walk the entire route should contact the sources listed for each of the sections for more detailed information.

The trail enters Michigan near Waldron in the southeastern portion of the state. The NCT meanders north and west through a series of urban and rural settings to reach certified segments of the trail through state game areas and state and national forests. Once the Lower Peninsula portion of the NCT approaches the Jordan River Valley, the trails take a decided northward path toward the Straits of Mackinac.

The Upper Peninsula's segment of the NCT is described in an east-to-west direction, starting in the Hiawatha National Forest adjacent to St. Ignace. The trail passes through the wilderness of the Upper Peninsula, into Tahquamenon Falls State Park, Pictured Rocks National Lakeshore, and the Ottawa National Forest before leaving Michigan through the city of Ironwood.

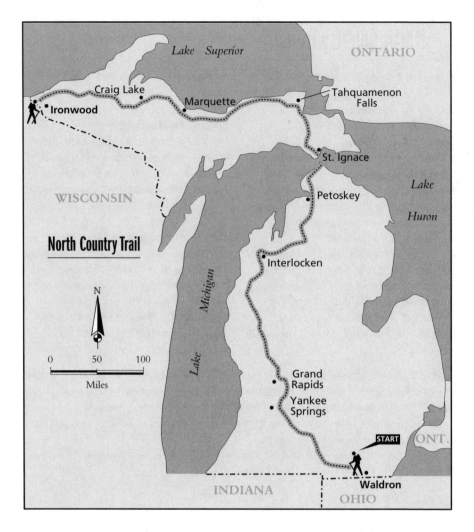

Descriptions of the trail are brief and general, since it would take—and, in fact, has taken—an entire book to complete. Hikers intending to explore either the entire length or bits and pieces of the NCT are encouraged to contact the references mentioned throughout this chapter.

Lower Peninsula

Not yet complete, the trailhead at the Ohio-Michigan border will eventually be located near the village of Waldron in Hillsdale County. Hikers can follow Waldron Road north for about 8 miles and then turn east onto Union Road for the 3-mile hike to the Lost Nations State Game Area. Here a stretch of uncertified trail will lead hikers northwest through Osseo and onto the Baw Beese Trail, Michigan's first stretch of certified trail in the NCT.

The trail passes through Hillsdale on a river trail and then follows the M–99 bicycle trail linking Hillsdale and Jonesville. The next 40 miles are a hiker's choice of county roads tracing the route to downtown Battle Creek and the 8-mile Linear Parkway and an interesting stop at Fort Custer National Cemetery, just 0.25 mile from Augusta, a great place to stop for the night. Hikers can find cabins for rent at the nearby lake. For information contact the Battle Creek Public Works Department, Battle Creek, MI 49014.

From the city of Augusta, the trail follows a 30-mile network of newly certified NCT trail, trails under development, and county roads through Kalamazoo and Barry Counties until you reach the next navigation point, Barry State Game Area and Yankee Springs State Park. Contact the Department of Natural Resources for information at the Yankee Springs Field Office, 2104 Gun Lake Road, Middleville, MI 48933.

Without good trails north of Barry County, hikers will be forced back onto county roads to reach Lowell in Kent County. There are a few certified miles of NCT trail in the Lowell State Game Area; a good county map will prove invaluable. North of the game area, hikers will again be on county roads until they reach the Rogue River State Game Area at the northwest corner of Kent County. No camping is permitted in the area, but there are 4.5 miles of NCT trail. Once in Newaygo County, hikers are nearing the first lengthy stretch of usable trail.

In Newaygo County, hikers will have to follow county roads to reach Croton Dam, a popular fishing spot for salmon and steelhead anglers, about 12 miles from the county line. Here the 115 miles of Manistee National Forest trails begin. Camping is available at Croton Dam Campground, 1 mile north of the dam.

Hikers will begin to notice a change in land ownership, switching to more public than private and, an added bonus, fairly clearly marked trails from here to the central Upper Peninsula. The pathway heads northwest for about 15 miles, crossing the White River Bridge just past Echo Road. There's a campground 1 mile to the west.

For more information contact the Forest Supervisor, Manistee National Forest, 421 South Mitchell Street, Cadillac, MI 49601.

There is a very special stopover for hikers 7 miles northwest of White Cloud. An easy 1.5-mile side trip from the trail leads to the NCT Schoolhouse Hostel in the Birch Grove School, once the headquarters of the NCT.

Hikers can pick up the trail from the hostel and again turn north for more than 15 miles until reaching the Nichols Lake Campground. From here it's a 2-mile hike to Highbank Lake and another small campground. Follow Forest Road 5541 and Star Lake Road to Carrs Road in Lake County.

From this checkpoint, hikers head northwest for 4 miles through Manistee National Forest to South Branch Road. The trail then winds north for 14 miles to Lake Road. Much of this leg of the NCT passes through public forest land, and camping is permitted 200 feet or more from the trail. Hikers will have to follow

Lake Road for 6 more miles until reaching Elk Highway, then take Campbell Road north and west for just over 10 miles to the Campbell Road bridge to cross the Little Manistee River and then travel 2 more miles to Forest Road 5337.

About 5 miles from the FR 5337 junction in Manistee County, the trail crosses Michigan Highway 55 and turns northeast for 1.5 miles to Pine Creek Road and the 2 miles to Chicago Road. From here it's only 2 more miles to High Bridge Road and the Manistee River crossing. The trail turns eastward for the next 4.5 hilly miles to Forest Road 5233, then north for 6 miles to Coates Road. Forest roads are the trail for the next 15 miles as hikers reach a roadside park just inside Wexford County. County roads will again make up the next 9 miles to Michigan Highway 37.

Once across M–37, the NCT parallels the north bank of the Manistee River until it reaches Baxter Bridge, a distance of about 15 miles. The terrain here changes dramatically and suddenly, and hikers at the end of their stamina will need frequent rests to navigate this stretch safely. There is a state forest campground just south of Baxter Bridge; watch for the signs near the bridge.

From this point the trail passes through a small segment of Wexford and Grand Traverse Counties before linking with the Shore-to-Shore Trail (see Hike 21), which it then follows for the next 55 miles.

The Shore-to-Shore Trail can be difficult for hikers, since the trail cuts through sandy and hilly terrain scarred by years of equestrian use. The route is clearly marked with a series of blue blazes featuring a footprint and a horseshoe. The trail is easy to follow, and there is camping along the route.

The North Country Trail passes through forest, urban areas, and farmland like this abandoned farm in northern lower Michigan.

The final leg of the Shore-to-Shore Trail ends at Magni Road in Kalkaska County, just after hikers ford the Boardman River. Horses find the crossing simple, but hikers can face a real challenge here, particularly in the spring or following a torrential rainfall. Sheck's Place, a state forest campground, is located at the river crossing.

Near the corner of Sunset Road and County Road 612, a link in the NCT splits to the east and eventually turns north for the 20-mile trek to the Jordan River Pathway, northwest of Alba. From here hikers will be linked with the Warner Creek Pathway and a series of stretches of certified trail mixed in with county roads as hikers pass north through Antrim and Charlevoix Counties and eventually into the city of Petoskey.

The NCT continues decidedly north from Petoskey, heading into Emmet County and toward the west shore of Wycamp Lake. From Wycamp Lake the trail heads north for about 1 mile into a state forest campground, then northwest for another mile to the Lake Michigan shore at Sturgeon Bay. Follow Lakeshore Road for 3 miles to the junction with Lakeview Road. From here it's only 2 more miles to Wilderness State Park. This is a great spot to camp and take a break from the rigors of the trail, especially with the Mackinac Bridge within sight. Hikers will find great campsites and even cabins to rent if they want to make an extended stay in the park.

For park information contact Wilderness State Park, Box 380, Carp Lake, MI 49718.

Hikers leave the park and follow Spruce Ridge Trail for about 2 miles to Cecil Bay Road. From here the trail winds through dense cedar forests until it links with an abandoned railroad grade leading into Mackinaw City.

Hikers approaching the Straits of Mackinac and the Mackinac Bridge from the south have only two options to get across to the Upper Peninsula: Call for the Mackinac Bridge Authority shuttle bus (906–643–7600), $2.00 per person; or hike into Mackinaw City and board one of the ferries running to Mackinac Island, transfer there onto a St. Ignace–bound ferry, and complete the trip to the Upper Peninsula.

Approaching the bridge from the north affords the same two options, but hikers reaching the Mackinac Bridge on Labor Day weekend can join the annual Mackinac Bridge Walk, led by Michigan's governor and his family. More than 60,000 "hikers" make the 5-mile hike each Labor Day. This, by the way, is the only legal way to walk across the Straits of Mackinac and into St. Ignace.

Upper Peninsula

Hikers dropped off at the north end of the Mackinac Bridge will walk through Straits State Park and on into St. Ignace to reach the abandoned Wisconsin Central Railroad grade leading to the first length of certified trail in the Upper Peninsula, at Castle Rock Road. The trail passes through old dunes, stands of red and white pines, and occasional views of the Lake Michigan shoreline. Excellent artesian water is available at Brevort Lake Park, across from Boedne Bay.

For information contact: Hiawatha National Forest, St. Ignace Ranger District, 1498 West U.S. 2, St. Ignace, MI 49781.

Hikers will cross the Brevort River on Brevort Camp Road. The trail picks up 0.2 mile north on the right side of the road and then winds through a large stand of red pine planted by the Civilian Conservation Corps in 1933. Nearly 0.5 mile north of the trail's junction with Worth Road, there is a small footbridge over Silver Creek. There are several terrain changes and habitat changes, ranging from hardwood forests to pine thickets, over the next few miles of trail.

The next section of the NCT crosses the Carp River, a remote area that can be quite wet in spring and early summer. From the Carp River the trail crosses Michigan Highway 123 and follows an abandoned railroad grade for nearly 0.5 mile before heading northwest just past Bissel Creek. The trail cuts a swath through the Mackinac Wilderness Area, a section of the NCT that virtually ensures hikers a better than average opportunity to see a variety of Michigan's wildlife, including bears and wolves.

Filterable water is available from the Carp River and at Trout Brook Pond.

About 1.8 miles north, the trail crosses Little Bear Creek over a 300-foot-long beaver dam. The footing can be tricky, so proceed with caution and the aid of a walking stick to steady your balance—and your nerves. There are wilderness-type campsites all along the trail, but remember to get at least 200 feet from the trail before setting up camp.

The next 18 miles of trail starts on the north side of Trout Brook Pond and is reached by walking through the parking area on the southeast edge of the pond. Hikers will have to cross a small, narrow dam, continue through a heavily forested area, and then parallel Biscuit Creek to Spur Road. Here the NCT follows narrow two-track roads to reach the next landmark, the Pine River Bridge. There is a primitive campsite at the bridge, but in fall you may have to share it with fishermen, hunters, and other outdoors-oriented folks.

From here the trail parallels the north side of Pine River, crossing Dick Road and, later, Lone Pine Road. The trail traces the edge of the Betchler Swamp for nearly 4 miles before it recrosses Dick Road and courses through a small stand of pines and opens onto Soldier Lake. Well water and camping are available at Soldier Lake.

The next segment of the NCT, a 13-mile trek from Soldier Lake to the mouth of Naomikong Creek, meanders through fairly rolling terrain that features both pine and hardwood forests. A network of boardwalks cross the lowland areas, often very wet for lengthy periods of time. An ADA-approved 100-foot suspension bridge crosses the creek. Filterable water is available from the creek or Lake Superior.

The trail leaves the Hiawatha National Forest, and hikers have the option of following the trail or walking the beach to Ankodosh Creek. The trail from here is certified for the next 3 miles to the boundary of Tahquamenon River State Park at M–123. At the M–123 crossing, the trail follows a snowmobile trail paralleling the east side of the highway, crossing the river near its mouth on Lake Superior.

A certified section of the trail resumes on the north side of the river and follows Tahquamenon Road for 5 miles to Cheney Creek. Since hikers are now in a state park, camping is a bit less than rustic; showers are available.

The NCT continues northwest to Culhane Lake and on to the mouth of the fabled Two Hearted River. This 26-mile section of the trail is well marked, and several links coincide with state park day-hike trails. The trail shadows the Tahquamenon River for a time before crossing M–123. From here the trail meanders along the east and west sides of Luce County Road 500 and crosses the Two Hearted River several times during the next 10 miles to the footbridge that marks the final crossing of the river and the beginning of the decidedly westward course of the NCT.

For information on the segment of the NCT from St. Ignace to the Two Hearted River, contact Kirt Stage-Harvey, Hiawatha Shore-to-Shore Chapter of the NCT, 950 Huron Street, St. Ignace, MI 49781.

The next 26 miles of the trail trace the Lake Superior shoreline before hikers turn south onto County Road H58 for a 3-mile hike into Grand Marais. From the village it's another 3 miles to the start of the 43-mile-long Pictured Rocks National Lakeshore Trail, the only major link under the control of the National Park Service. The trail shadows the shoreline, passing cliffs and sand dunes, before reaching the end of this link at Munising Falls.

Contact the Park Superintendent, Pictured Rocks National Lakeshore, P.O. Box 40, Munising, MI 49862.

From the falls, hikers will have to follow county and state highways for the next 3 miles to reconnect with the NCT off Michigan Highway 94. The next 24 miles of trail follow a network of forest roads, crossing the Au Train River at the bridge on Forest Road 2276 and later crossing the Laughing Whitefish River along the same road. It is another 4 miles to the trail junction with Michigan Highway 28 and then west to the paved bike path that leads into the city of Marquette.

Information on this segment of the trail is available by contacting the Hiawatha National Forest, Munising Ranger District, 400 Munising Street, Munising, MI 49862.

Since the NCT is still under development in this area and throughout north-central Marquette County, hikers are advised to obtain good county maps and follow M–28 from Silver Lake Basin to Craig Lake State Park, a distance of approximately 18 miles. Camping is permitted in the park as long as you set up more than 150 feet from any lakeshore.

For information on this segment of the trail, contact North Country Trail Hikers Club, 12 Middle Island Point, Marquette, MI 49855.

From Craig Lake State Park, hikers should follow M–28 for another 5 miles until reaching the junction with Vermilac Road. The trailhead for the next segment of the NCT is 5 miles from the junction to the Plain Road bridge over the Sturgeon River. The trail shadows the north bank of the river and for about the next 25 miles traces the rim of the Sturgeon River Valley and a small portion of the Ottawa National Forest.

For information on the Ottawa National Forest, contact Ottawa National Forest, 2100 East Cloverland Drive, Ironwood, MI 49938.

Hikers will have to wade the East Branch of the Ontonagon River near Gardner Road. If the river is high, particularly in spring, or you just want to keep your feet dry, take the 3-mile detour along forest roads. A serious warning for campers: This is black bear country, and gray wolves are increasingly making their presence felt and seen. Exercise caution, and take all necessary precautions to avoid encounters with either animal.

From Gardner Road, the NCT heads west again, this time for the 7-mile trek to U.S. Highway 45 to a spot near Victoria Dam on the Ontonagon River. If the dam is releasing water, the crossing is a rock-hopper's pleasure cruise; if the water is high, do *not* attempt to cross the river. Instead follow U.S. 45 and local roadways through Rockland to reach the other bank. West of this point, the trail is about as rugged as the NCT gets in Michigan, and the next nearly 30 miles will test the stamina of any hiker.

About 12 miles farther west, the trail crosses the Gogebic Ridge Trail; 4 miles to the northwest, the trail reaches the Michigan Highway 64 crossing. The trail then turns north for about 3 miles, crosses the Big Iron River, and then follows the north bank of the West Branch of the Big Iron River for about 8 miles until the NCT reaches the boundary of Porcupine Mountains State Park.

For information on this next segment of the NCT, contact the Park Supervisor, Porcupine Mountains State Park, Route 314, Ontonagon, MI 49953. Hikers must register at park headquarters before venturing into the park's interior.

Two small trails, Lily Pond and South Carp River Trails, lead to the Lake Superior lakeshore. Hikers follow the lakeshore to County Road 519. About 4 miles farther, the NCT crosses Forest Road 117 and then follows a meandering trace for 5 miles to the Black River Campground. From the campground the trail shadows the west bank of the Black River for the 5-mile trek to Copper Peak Hill. Then it's 6 miles south on County Road 513, 8 miles to Auvignon Corner, and on into the city of Ironwood.

To reach the NCT trailhead in Wisconsin, follow U.S. 2 across the Montreal River. The trailhead is adjacent to the bridge.

Isle Royale National Park

sle Royale is the largest freshwater island in the United States. In north-central Lake Superior, some 70 miles north of Houghton, Michigan, 49 miles north of Copper Harbor, Michigan, and 22 miles east of Grand Portage, Minnesota, it is still remote and wild. Access to the park is limited to air or water, so the stormy waters of Lake Superior can delay arrivals and departures. Allow a little latitude in your timetable when planning a trip to this isolated wilderness.

Isle Royale National Park was authorized by the U.S. Congress in 1931 "to conserve a prime example of Northwoods Wilderness." The park was designated part of the National Wilderness Preservation System in 1976, under the Wilderness Act, and today remains an example of primitive America. In 1981 Isle Royale was designated a Biosphere Reserve by the United Nations, recognizing the park's international significance. The park is made up of one large island and more than 400 smaller islands. The main island, the namesake of the park, is 45 miles long and nearly 9 miles wide at its widest point.

As much as 99 percent of the park has been designated as wilderness under the aegis of the National Park Service. The rugged nature of the terrain makes this one of the most picturesque settings a hiker could hope for. The park's outstanding isolation is protected by the island's location and makes it an ideal natural laboratory; wolves and moose have been studied on Isle Royale for more than three decades in the longest ongoing wildlife study anywhere in the world. The island supports populations of raptors, such as eagles, peregrine falcons, and ospreys, and large numbers of waterfowl. Fishing enthusiasts find plenty of action in inland lakes and along offshore reefs; photographers are sometimes overwhelmed by the opportunities here. Add to these natural wonders the relics of early attempts to commercialize the island's resources—ancient copper mines and more—and you have a spectacular trip in store.

Approximately 165 miles of trails crisscross the 200-square-mile island. Hikes range from comfortable day hikes to cross-island excursions not recommended for anyone lacking experience, stamina, and, most important, the proper equipment. Since just getting to the island requires a level of commitment, the hikes in the park

Isle Royale National Park, a stark-rock respite from the watery expanse of Lake Superior, consists of one large island surrounded by nearly 400 small rocky outcrops.

are rated as comfortably moderate to difficult, with a majority of the hikes falling midway between the two. The island's trail systems are well defined and easy to follow, with the exception of the Minong Ridge Trail, which offers a challenge to even seasoned hikers. Hikers on Isle Royale are limited primarily by time and determination—how willing they are to experience the wilderness.

The Isle Royale Topographic Map, sold in the region, is a more than adequate guide for hikers, but a number of specialized booklets are available locally, including *Isle Royale National Park,* by Jim DuFresne, which may assist first-time visitors. The staff at each of the visitor centers on the island can answer most questions.

Trail time estimates for Isle Royale have to be tempered with the unpredictable weather of the region. Most hikers will be able to maintain a 2-mile-per-hour pace, despite influences of constantly changing weather patterns caused by Lake Superior. In early summer, bugs can be a real problem in remote corners of the island. The later months of summer are the best months for hikers on the island, but it frequently rains during these warmer months, so be prepared. Daytime temperatures are often pleasant, and sometimes very warm, but nights can be cool, even chilly.

During fall, evening temperatures can dip to nearly freezing. The park is open to visitors from mid-April until late October, so if visiting Isle Royale doesn't fit your summer vacation schedule, there is still plenty of time to hike the island's backcountry.

Elevations on the island are not a major factor on most hikes, although a tired hiker facing a steep 15- to 20-foot climb might argue the point. Major elevations are encountered along the Greenstone Ridge Trail, though. The six highest points are Sugar Mountain (1,362 feet), Mount Desor (1,394 feet), Ishpeming Point (1,377 feet), Mount Siskiwit (1,205 feet), Mount Ojibway (1,136 feet), and Mount Franklin (1,074 feet).

Off-trail travel is difficult on Isle Royale, since vegetation is thick and marshy areas make shortcuts nearly impossible to navigate. The fragile environment of the island has led to implementation of a low-impact camping policy in the park's thirty-six campgrounds. The guidelines for the policy are simply this: Leave only footprints. Do not exaggerate your presence while hiking the park's trails. Remember, you are a visitor—an intruder—to the ecosystem.

Trailheads for the hikes around the island are, for all intents and purposes, the ferry docks that carry passengers from either Michigan or Minnesota to the island. The ferries make regular stops in various locations, providing access to the entire island so that hikers do not have to make lengthy cross-country treks. From Houghton, the *Ranger III* makes regular stops at the eastern landfall of Rock Harbor. At this landing, hikers will find an information center, meals, lodging, groceries, and other services, such as boat rentals. The *Isle Royale Queen III* sails from Copper Harbor, stopping also at Rock Harbor. The *Voyageur II,* sailing from Grand Portage, Minnesota, makes regular stops at Windigo, McCargoe Cove, Belle Isle, Rock Harbor, Daisy Farm, Chippewa Harbor, and Malone Bay. A second vessel, the *Wenonah,* also sails from Grand Portage but has scheduled stops only at Windigo.

Other options are available through watercraft charters if you want to customize your visit to the park. For more information, contact National Park Concessions, Inc. at (906) 337–4993.

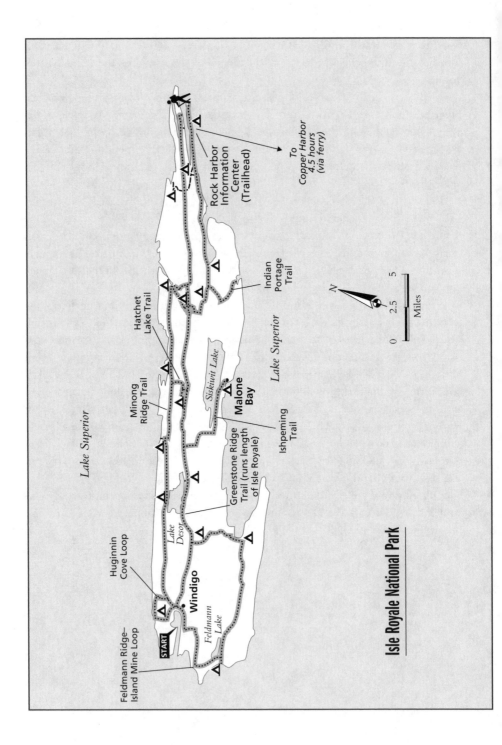

Isle Royale National Park

2 Greenstone Ridge Trail

Highlights: The park's most extensive trail, following the backbone of the island along its highest ridges.

Type of hike: Backpack linear hike.

Total distance: 40 miles.

Difficulty: Difficult.

Best months: The park is open mid-April to late October.

Map: Isle Royale Topographic Map.

Permits and fees: Hikers heading for Isle Royale have two choices to reach the remote serenity of this island park: 4 to 6 hours in a boat or half that time in a floatplane. From Houghton it's a 6.5-hour ride aboard the *Ranger III*, a 165-foot vessel and a round-trip fare of $47. From Copper Harbor the ride is 4.5 hours aboard the *Isle Royale Queen III*, an 81-foot vessel and a round-trip fare of $80. For those in a hurry, Isle Royale Seaplane Service will fly hikers to the island at a rate of $149 each way.

Once on the island, a second option exists: Operated by the park concessionaire, a ferryboat stops at several drop-off points that can turn a loop hike into a linear one. One-way rates range from $80 to $150 per person.

There is also a $4.00 per person park entrance fee.

Special considerations: Once ashore, there is no turning back. In spring and early summer, bugs can add an aerobic element to your hike; if that is a factor you would just as soon avoid, travel in late summer and early fall.

For more information: Park Superintendent, Isle Royale National Park, 87 North Ripley Street, Houghton, MI 49931.

Parking and trailhead facilities: Hikers are advised to bring everything they need with them, since there is little opportunity to shop and what's available is expensive.

Finding the trailhead: Ride the concessionaire's shuttle ferry to Windigo at the west end of Isle Royale and you will be put ashore at the western trailhead. The eastern trailhead is located at Lookout Louise, a short hike from Rock Harbor.

The hike:

The "Greenstone," as it's called here, is rated by many as the best of the Isle Royale hikes. The trail goes from Windigo, in the west, to Lookout Louise, in the east, traversing 40 miles of rugged beauty along the highest ridges of Isle Royale.

From the trailhead at Windigo, the trail rises to the first campground at Island Mine Campground, 6.3 miles to the east. The initial section of the trail is also the toughest of the entire trip; over the next 5.5 miles, hikers climb to the crest of Sugar Mountain (1,362 feet). The Island Mine Campground is a welcome sight after this ambitious start. To reach the campground you will have to make a 0.4-mile detour south onto the Island Mine Trail. The junction and the trail are well marked and easy to follow. Rest here; there's more work ahead.

Back on the main trail, hikers face a second steep ascent as they head for Mount Desor (1,394 feet), the highest elevation on the island, 1.5 miles east. Just over 3.5 miles east of this peak is the junction with a 0.25-mile spur trail running north to Lake Desor Campground.

The island is home to a number of bald eagles and other birdlife along the shoreline and the interior regions.

The next leg of the trail, from Lake Desor to Hatchet Lake, is 8 miles long, and it's not flat. Hikers must scale yet another peak, Ishpeming Point (1,377 feet). The crest marks the halfway point of this leg—with the first half being the easier of the two. An observation tower marks the summit, but don't hope for much of a view around the island's thick foliage. Hikers have compared the final 4 miles of the Desor-Hatchet leg to a long roller-coaster ride that makes the next campground a welcome sight. For the most part, thick forest blocks many of the views, even though you are hiking along the backbone of the park. Weary hikers finally reach the spur trail to the next campground on the shores of Hatchet Lake; the spur heads north off the main trail and goes for 0.5 mile.

The next leg of the trail includes still another peak, Mount Siskiwit (1,205 feet), but hikers won't have to climb it. That's little compensation, though—it's tough terrain along this trek to West Chickenbone Campground, nearly 8 miles east. The trail is not easy and will probably be the longest 8 miles you have hiked in some time. A satisfying element of this leg is that the views are quite good. The descent into the campground is fairly steep, dropping into a heavily forested area before reaching the junction with the campground spur trail.

Less than 2 miles farther east is the East Chickenbone Campground, so if the previous day's jaunt caused you to oversleep a bit, the next campground is just ahead—after all, some progress is better than none. The campground at East Chickenbone also marks the junction with the Minong Ridge Trail and the route to McCargoe Cove to the north.

From here on, the trail is fairly easy, although low-lying areas along the way have been known to spawn plenty of bugs in spring and early summer. It is about 4.5 miles to the a spur trail to the south, which leads to the Daisy Farm Campground. The 1.9-mile hike in is fairly easy; after a good night's sleep, hikers take a 1.7-mile hike along another spur trail that leads back to the main Greenstone route. The second spur trail rejoins the main trail at Mount Ojibway (1,136 feet). It is a fairly flat 2-mile hike to the final high point, Mount Franklin (1,074 feet). From here it is an easy 4.8 miles to the eastern trailhead at Lookout Louise.

Hikers who have completed the Greenstone cross-island trek have two options: Arrange ahead of time for a boat to transport them across Tobin Harbor, or backtrack to the junction with the Tobin Harbor Trail for a hike into Rock Harbor.

Key points (west to east):

5.5   Sugar Mountain

6.3   Island Mine Campground

7.8   Mount Desor

15.3 Ishpeming Point

19.3 Hatchet Lake Campground

27.3 West Chickenbone Campground

33.7 Daisy Farm Campground

40.0 Lookout Louise

3 Minong Ridge Trail

Highlights: A cross-island hike along Minong Ridge to the Minong Mine and McCargoe Cove.

Type of hike: Backpack linear hike.

Total distance: 29 miles.

Difficulty: Difficult.

Best months: The park is open mid-April to late October.

Map: Isle Royale Topographic Map.

Permits and fees: Hikers heading for Isle Royale have two choices to reach the remote serenity of this island park: 4 to 6 hours in a boat or half that time in a floatplane. From Houghton it's a 6.5-hour ride aboard the *Ranger III*, a 165-foot vessel and a round-trip fare of $47. From Copper Harbor the ride is 4.5 hours aboard the *Isle Royale Queen III*, an 81-foot vessel and a round-trip fare of $80. For those in a hurry, Isle Royale Seaplane Service will fly hikers to the island at a rate of $149 each way.

Once on the island, a second option exists: Operated by the park concessionaire, a ferry-boat stops at several drop-off points that can turn a loop hike into a linear one. One-way rates range from $80 to $150 per person.

There is also a $4.00 per person park entrance fee.

Special considerations: Boggy wet areas spawn plenty of bugs in spring and early summer. Hiking the hard rock ridge will quickly test your footwear. Be certain your boots can stand the test.

For more information: Park Superintendent, Isle Royale National Park, 87 North Ripley Street, Houghton, MI 49931.

Parking and trailhead facilities: There is a good landing spot, but that's the extent of the creature comforts.

(See map on page 28.)

Finding the trailhead: The concessionaire's shuttle ferry will provide access to the trailhead at McCargoe Cove and serve as your pickup boat at the end of the hike at Windigo.

The hike:

Starting at the eastern trailhead at McCargoe Cove is the gentle way to start this relatively difficult cross-island trek. From here, the first campground at Todd Harbor is a mere 6.6 miles west.

The first 4 miles of this leg more or less follow the rocky ridgelines; hiking can be difficult and the trail sometimes tough to keep track of. About 2 miles from the campground, the trail leaves the ridgelines and drops into a thick forested area. The roller coaster doesn't stop, but the trail is more shaded.

The second segment is a bit less strenuous. Its initial 1.5 miles are actually quite pleasant until you pass the junction with the Hatchet Lake Trail. Here you become a ridge walker again, and, although the trail is not nearly as imposing as the first leg, you will feel the same soreness by the end of the day. The final section of this part of the trail is a 0.5-mile descent to the campground at Little Todd Harbor. Look out for boggy areas, especially after a good rainfall.

Like a welcome respite, the third leg of the Minong Ridge Trail is a brief 6-mile trek to the next stop at Lake Desor Campground. Hikers will spend nearly equal amounts of time along ridgelines and in forested areas as they continue westward. The trail does contain its share of ups and downs, but after nearly 6 miles the final descent starts at the junction with the spur trail leading to the campground 0.5 mile south of the main pathway.

The final 13 miles of trail are not terribly difficult, although they do require some special navigating through the wet areas. Ridge-hopping is somewhat less strenuous here, but it's the length of this part of the hike that takes the greatest toll on stamina. Hikers will pass several junctions with the east and west ends of the Huginnin Cove Loop and, later, will merge with the Greenstone before ending at Windigo.

Hikers anxious to get deep into the backcountry can start the hike at its western trailhead (Windigo), but prepare for a 12-mile hike to the first campground at Lake Desor, or opt for the hike north on the Huginnin Cove Trail and the campground there, about 5 miles from the trailhead. Keep in mind that if you choose to layover at Huginnin that first night, you will have another 5-mile hike facing you in the morning before you rejoin the Minong Ridge Trail.

Key points:

6.6 Todd Harbor Campground
11.0 Little Todd Harbor Campground
16.0 Lake Desor Campground
29.0 Windigo

4 Feldmann Ridge–Island Mine Loop

Highlights: A scenic loop hike tracing the southwest corner of this island park.

Type of hike: Backpack loop hike.

Total distance: 28 miles.

Difficulty: Moderate to difficult.

Best months: The park is open mid-April to late October.

Map: Isle Royale Topographic Map.

Permits and fees: Hikers heading for Isle Royale have two choices to reach the remote serenity of this island park: 4 to 6 hours in a boat or half that time in a floatplane. From Houghton it's a 6.5-hour ride aboard the *Ranger III,* a 165-foot vessel and a round-trip fare of $47. From Copper Harbor the ride is 4.5 hours aboard the *Isle Royale Queen III,* an 81-foot vessel and a round-trip fare of $80. For those in a hurry, Isle Royale Seaplane Service will fly hikers to the island at a rate of $149 each way.

Once on the island, a second option exists: Operated by the park concessionaire, a ferryboat stops at several drop-off points that can turn a loop hike into a linear one. One-way rates range from $80 to $150 per person.

There is also a $4.00 per person park entrance fee.

Special considerations: Boggy wet areas spawn plenty of bugs in spring and early summer. Hiking the hard rock ridge will quickly test your footwear. Be certain your boots can stand the test.

For more information: Park Superintendent, Isle Royale National Park, 87 North Ripley Street, Houghton, MI 49931.

Parking and trailhead facilities: There is a good landing spot, but that's the extent of the creature comforts.

(See map on page 28.)

Finding the trailhead: The trailhead at Windigo is the start and finish line for this loop hike.

The hike:

This 24-mile loop is a mildly rugged trail that traces the southwest corner of the park, an area with few tough stretches and plenty of scenery. Most of the trek is along fairly level trails, but hikers should prepare for two tough sections over Greenstone and Feldmann Ridges, with the latter being the toughest.

From Windigo, hikers head generally west and then south for a 9-mile hike to the campground at Feldmann Lake. The first 5.5 miles of the hike go through a marshy area frequented by the island's largest resident, the moose. The final few miles to the campground provide occasional glimpses of Rainbow Cove. With 0.5 mile to go, hikers will catch sight of their destination.

The trek from Feldmann Lake to Siskiwit Bay could be a hiker's toughest full day spent on the island. The 10.2-mile leg of this loop includes 5 miles of tough hiking along Feldmann Ridge. From Feldmann Lake Campground, the first 1.5 miles spent ascending the ridge are typical of what is ahead—a steep rise that pretty much sets the pattern for the next 5 miles. An observation tower located about midway along the ridge is a welcome rest area; you are about halfway through the tough part of the ridge, and halfway through this tough section of the hike as well. Nearly 2 miles east of the tower you begin the long descent to Siskiwit Bay. After hiking this section, it's not at all uncommon to give in to the urge to linger for an extra day, especially knowing that a tough hike along the Greenstone Ridge is just a few miles north.

The short 4.8 miles to the junction with the Greenstone Ridge Trail is a walk through the mining history of Isle Royale. Hikers pass the remains of many of the buildings and, near the end, the signs of the mine that gives its name to the trail, Island Mine. Just after leaving the mine, hikers face a steep ascent to Red Oak Ridge, at an elevation of more than 1,200 feet. After a few more yards, the Island Mine Campground comes into view. Depending on their conditioning, hikers can either choose to stay here for the night or immediately hike the 6.5 downhill miles along the Greenstone back to Windigo.

Key points:

9.0 Feldmann Lake Campground

17.2 Siskiwit Bay

22.0 Island Mine Campground

28.0 Windigo

5 Rock Harbor Trail

Highlights: One of the park's most popular short hikes, offering scenic shoreline views and campsites near the island's inland lakes.

Type of hike: Backpack linear hike.

Total distance: 13 miles.

Difficulty: Moderate.

Best months: The park is open mid-April to late October.

Map: Isle Royale Topographic Map.

Permits and fees: Hikers heading for Isle Royale have two choices to reach the remote serenity of this island park: 4 to 6 hours in a boat or half that time in a floatplane. From Houghton it's a 6.5-hour ride aboard the *Ranger III,* a 165-foot vessel and a round-trip fare of $47. From Copper Harbor the ride is 4.5 hours aboard the *Isle Royale Queen III,* an 81-foot vessel and a round-trip fare of $80. For those in a hurry, Isle Royale Seaplane Service will fly hikers to the island at a rate of $149 each way.

Once on the island, a second option exists: Operated by the park concessionaire, a ferryboat stops at several drop-off points that can turn a loop hike into a linear one. One-way rates range from $80 to $150 per person.

There is also a $4.00 per person park entrance fee.

Special considerations: Boggy wet areas spawn plenty of bugs in spring and early summer. Hiking the hard rock ridge will quickly test your footwear. Be certain your boots can stand the test.

For more information: Park Superintendent, Isle Royale National Park, 87 North Ripley Street, Houghton, MI 49931.

Parking and trailhead facilities: There is a good landing spot, but that's the extent of the creature comforts.

(See map on page 28.)

Finding the trailhead: The trailhead is at the park concessionaire's dock in Rock Harbor.

The hike:

According to park officials, this trail is probably the most heavily used trail on the island. Experienced hikers could go its entire length in just a couple of days, but the few obstacles along the way would challenge the casual hiker.

The legs of the hike, like those of most other hikes on the island, are measured by the distances between possible campsites. The first stop at Three-Mile Campground should confuse no one when asking how far it is. This initial section is an easy-to-follow trail that can be somewhat treacherous after a rain.

The second day on the trail beings with a 4.4-mile hike to Daisy Farm Campground. This section is relatively easy and has the added bonus of providing some remarkable offshore scenery. About halfway along this leg, hikers will pass what's left of the Siskiwit Mine. From the mine site, it's another 2 miles to the campground.

The third day, 4 miles of the Rock Harbor Trail, ends at Moskey Basin and its campground. The path follows the Daisy Farm Trail for 0.2 mile before the trails split. The Rock Harbor Trail continues on, following the terrain as it parallels the shoreline of Moskey Basin around to the campground.

From this point the trail continues for nearly 2 miles to Lake Richie, where it ends.

Key points:

3.0 Three-Mile Campground

5.5 Siskiwit Mine

7.4 Daisy Farm Campground

11.4 Moskey Basin Campground

12.9 Lake Richie

6 Indian Portage Trail

Highlights: A trail over a historic Native American portage route from McCargoe Cove to Chippewa Harbor.

Type of hike: Linear hike.

Total distance: 11 miles.

Difficulty: Moderate.

Best months: The park is open mid-April to late October.

Map: Isle Royale Topographic Map.

Permits and fees: Hikers heading for Isle Royale have two choices to reach the remote serenity of this island park: 4 to 6 hours in a boat or half that time in a floatplane. From Houghton it's a 6.5-hour ride aboard the *Ranger III,* a 165-foot vessel and a round-trip fare of $47. From Copper Harbor the ride is 4.5 hours aboard the *Isle Royale Queen III,* an 81-foot vessel and a round-trip fare of $80. For those in a hurry, Isle Royale Seaplane Service will fly hikers to the island at a rate of $149 each way.

Once on the island, a second option exists: Operated by the park concessionaire, a ferryboat stops at several drop-off points that can turn a loop hike into a linear one. One-way rates range from $80 to $150 per person.

There is also a $4.00 per person park entrance fee.

Special considerations: Boggy wet areas spawn plenty of bugs in spring and early summer. Hiking the hard rock ridge will quickly test your footwear. Be certain your boots can stand the test.

For more information: Park Superintendent, Isle Royale National Park, 87 North Ripley Street, Houghton, MI 49931.

Parking and trailhead facilities: Services and amenities are what's available from your backpack.

(See map on page 28.)

Finding the trailhead: The trailhead is at the McCargoe Cove Campground.

The hike:

Islanders named this trail because of historic use by Native Americans to portage canoes along the route from Chippewa Harbor north to McCargoe Cove. The route traces portions of the shorelines of four inland lakes on its way to the sheltered waters of McCargoe Cove. Not a difficult hike, the trail has varied terrain that will slow many hikers. Allow for a long day to enjoy this 11-mile trail.

From the junction with the Minong Ridge Trail at the McCargoe Cove Campground, the trail heads south, tracing the western shores of Chickenbone Lake till it joins the Greenstone Ridge Trail. Only the final 0.2 mile before the Greenstone junction presents any obstacles—and this is a steep climb.

From the Greenstone, the trail continues south around the western edges of Lakes Livermore and LeSage. Here the trail switches and is routed around the eastern edge of Lake Richie. It then follows the course of the stream flowing out of the lake until it reaches Chippewa Harbor. There are several ascents along this leg of the trail, plus several marshy areas known to provide plenty of bugs during the season. From the mouth of the stream at Chippewa Harbor Campground to the end of the trail is about 0.5 mile east.

Key points:

This day hike traces a route around Chickenbone, Livermore, LeSage, and Richie Lakes before shadowing a stream for the final leg to Chippewa Harbor Campground.

7 Huginnin Cove Loop

Highlights: An optional loop off the Minong Ridge Trail to a picturesque shoreline campground.

Type of hike: Loop hike.

Total distance: 6.5 miles.

Difficulty: Easy to moderate.

Best months: The park is open mid-April to late October.

Map: Isle Royale Topographic Map.

Permits and fees: Hikers heading for Isle Royale have two choices to reach the remote serenity of this island park: 4 to 6 hours in a boat or half that time in a floatplane. From Houghton it's a 6.5-hour ride aboard the *Ranger III*, a 165-foot vessel and a round-trip fare of $47. From Copper Harbor the ride is 4.5 hours aboard the *Isle Royale Queen III*, an 81-foot vessel and a round-trip fare of $80. For those in a hurry, Isle Royale Seaplane Service will fly hikers to the island at a rate of

$149 each way.

Once on the island, a second option exists: Operated by the park concessionaire, a ferryboat stops at several drop-off points that can turn a loop hike into a linear one. One-way rates range from $80 to $150 per person.

There is also a $4.00 per person park entrance fee.

Special considerations: Boggy wet areas spawn plenty of bugs in spring and early summer. Hiking the hard rock ridge will quickly test your footwear. Be certain your boots can stand the test.

For more information: Park Superintendent, Isle Royale National Park, 87 North Ripley Street, Houghton, MI 49931.

Parking and trailhead facilities: Services and amenities are what's available from your backpack.

(See map on page 28.)

Finding the trailhead: The trailhead is near Washington Creek as it crosses the Minong Ridge Trail.

The hike:

This 6.5-mile loop is used as a warm-up by hikers preparing for the rugged Minong Ridge Trail—the picturesque campground in Huginnin Cove is an easy 3-hour hike from the Windigo ferry and makes a good first-night stopping place. The lowlands and swamps along this loop also provide hikers with an excellent opportunity to see moose and other wildlife.

The trail starts out on the Minong Ridge Trail. Hikers cross Washington Creek to reach the western trailhead for the loop several hundred yards after the creek crossing. The Huginnin Trail heads generally north from the junction for 3.1 miles to the campground on the cove.

The hike back to the Minong Ridge Trail goes about 3.3 miles along the eastern half of the loop, following the Lake Superior shoreline briefly before turning south through a marshy area. The remains of several cabins and the ill-fated Windigo Mine community are still visible along the trail. From here it is just yards to the junction with the Minong Ridge pathway.

Key points:

3.1 Huginnin Cove Campground
6.5 Junction with Minong Ridge Trail

8 Ishpeming Trail

Highlights: This trail connects Malone Bay with the Greenstone Ridge Trail at Ishpeming Point.

Type of hike: Backpack linear hike.

Total distance: 7 miles.

Difficulty: Moderate.

Best months: The park is open mid-April to late October.

Map: Isle Royale Topographic Map.

Permits and fees: Hikers heading for Isle Royale have two choices to reach the remote serenity of this island park: 4 to 6 hours in a boat or half that time in a floatplane. From Houghton it's a 6.5-hour ride aboard the *Ranger III*, a 165-foot vessel and a round-trip fare of $47. From Copper Harbor the ride is 4.5 hours aboard the *Isle Royale Queen III*, an 81-foot vessel and a round-trip fare of $80. For those in a hurry, Isle Royale Seaplane Service will fly hikers to the island at a rate of $149 each way.

Once on the island, a second option exists: Operated by the park concessionaire, a ferry-boat stops at several drop-off points that can turn a loop hike into a linear one. One-way rates range from $80 to $150 per person.

There is also a $4.00 per person park entrance fee.

Special considerations: Boggy wet areas spawn plenty of bugs in spring and early summer. Hiking the hard rock ridge will quickly test your footwear. Be certain your boots can stand the test.

For more information: Park Superintendent, Isle Royale National Park, 87 North Ripley Street, Houghton, MI 49931.

Parking and trailhead facilities: Services and amenities are what's available from your backpack.

(See map on page 28.)

Finding the trailhead: The trailhead is the ferry dock in Malone Bay.

The hike:

There are three steep climbs along the route, including the steepest climb of all—the trek to the peak of Ishpeming Point.

The trail can be hiked from the junction with the Greenstone (north to south) or from the ferry dock at Malone Bay (south to north). From the Greenstone trail-head the hike is all downhill, but you have to rely on water transportation once you reach the end of the trail to get you to your next destination. The hike from south to north is more difficult but allows more flexibility in planning connecting hikes.

From Malone Bay the trail traces the southern shores of Siskiwit Lake for more than 3 miles before it turns decidedly north and begins to climb. The trail's first major ascent, to Red Oak Ridge, is a 1-mile rise to an elevation of 1,088 feet.

The next 2.5 miles are real knee-benders: a quick descent off Red Oak Ridge into a marshy lowland, followed quickly by a climb to the second ridgeline that tops out at 1,123 feet. After one more descent, it's a quick climb to Ishpeming Point. From the point, campgrounds are located at Lake Desor to the west and Hatchet Lake to the east.

Key points:

3.0 Siskiwit Lake

4.0 Red Oak Ridge

6.5 Ishpeming Point

Honorable Mentions

Stoll Trail This easy two-hour, 4.3-mile hike from the Rock Harbor Lodge traces the finger of rock east of the lodge, leading to Scoville Point. The trail is fairly level and poses no special problems for even the casual hiker. Hikers will get a great view of not only Lake Superior but also Tobin Harbor and may even catch a glimpse of historic copper mining sites near the lodge.

It is nearly 2 miles to Scoville Point from the lodge; the trail is easy to follow. The return trip requires retracing your steps for 0.5 mile, then heading along the southern edge of Tobin Harbor to get back to the lodge.

This trail offers a great after-dinner hike or just a chance to stretch your legs while you wait for the ferry back to the mainland.

Tobin Harbor Trail This 3-mile linear route is an easy hike along the shoreline. It is an easy day hike from the lodge in Rock Harbor or a good jumping-off point for longer treks, including the Greenstone. The trail is wide and easy to follow, offering no special problems for hikers at any level of experience. The short trail ends at the junction with the Mount Franklin Trail.

Hatchet Lake Trail This 2.6-mile connector trail links Minong Ridge with the Greenstone Ridge Trail and provides access to Hatchet Lake Campground. The short trail is not an easy trek, however, because of a moderate number of quick climbs and stream crossings, regardless of which end you choose to start from.

From the Greenstone junction, the trails drops elevation quickly, reaching the shore of Hatchet Lake in about 0.3 mile. The trail curves east around the end of the lake before swinging back north to join the Minong Ridge Trail. This final section of the trail includes the roughest terrain and stream crossings. The campground at Todd Harbor is a bit under 1.5 miles east of the Minong Ridge Trail junction.

Lane Cove Trail The Lane Cove Trail is a 2.5-mile spur trail to Lane Cove Campground that offers hikers a respite from the Greenstone or an alternative start to that long trek westward along the ridge. Either way, it is easily reached from the Greenstone Ridge Trail, just east of the summit of Mount Franklin, or from Rock Harbor by means of the Tobin Harbor and Mount Franklin Trails.

From the junction with the Greenstone, the trail descends from the ridge and drops into a fairly wet area as it snakes north toward Lane Cove. The hike can be tough if the trail is wet, but a little caution along steeper sections will help. Hiking the 2.5 miles to the campground shouldn't take longer than a couple of hours.

Mount Franklin Trail Hikers using this 2-mile trail usually make their appearance from the south, at Three-Mile Campground, or from the east, on the Tobin Harbor Trail. Hikers coming from the north are generally winding up their west-to-east hike along the Greenstone and are bound for Rock Harbor and its ferry dock.

Leaving Three-Mile Campground, south-originating hikers will first go west for 0.15 mile to the junction with the Mount Franklin Trail, then north toward its junction with the Tobin Harbor Trail, about 0.5 mile later. The terrain in the area means lots of ups and downs—mostly ups. Waiting at the end of the hike is the climb to the crest of Greenstone Ridge, leaving the worst for last if you make the hike from the south.

The trail tops out just east of Mount Franklin and its 1,074-foot crest.

Daisy Farm Trail The 2-mile Daisy Farm Trail is mentioned in the Greenstone Ridge Trail description; it is the western approach to the campground at the Greenstone's southern terminus at Rock Harbor. This spur trail provides relief from the rigors of the Greenstone but by no means is rated an easy hike. This is due to the rough terrain leading to and from the campground. The scenery is great, but be prepared to do some climbing.

Ojibway Trail The 1.7-mile Ojibway Trail is the eastern leg of the route followed by many hikers making their way back to the Greenstone from the Daisy Farm Campground. The return trail is still steep but does not compare with the terrain along the Daisy Farm Trail to the west.

East Chickenbone Trail This 1.6-mile trail is a unique mix of terrain and habitats, offering an alternative route to the Minong Ridge and Greenstone Ridge Trails. It also provides a pathway around the eastern shores of Chickenbone Lake. The trail traces the eastern shores of the lake before heading cross-country to join the Indian Portage Trail for the trek to McCargoe Cove. The few brief climbs and descents here offer nothing overly challenging.

Windigo Nature Trail The shortest trail on the island, this 1.2-mile nature hike follows a twelve-stop self-guided route near the harbor at Windigo. A brochure available at the visitor center outlines each of the stops and provides all the information you need to enjoy this brief and scenic hike.

Porcupine Mountains Wilderness State Park

Michigan's Porcupine Wilderness State Park is the largest of the state's parks, covering nearly 60,000 acres in Ontonagon and Gogebic Counties. The park is one of the most visited in Michigan, but few visitors venture more than a few yards from their cars; most stay only long enough to snap a few photographs of the incredible vistas seen from scenic overlooks. Although a drive through the remote northern fringes of Michigan's Upper Peninsula sets the mood for a visit to this unique expanse of virgin forest and undisturbed shoreline, there is only one way to see what this park has to offer—travel on foot!

Porcupine Mountains Wilderness State Park stretches 25 miles along southern Lake Superior and inland for nearly 10 miles to include four major lakes, numerous streams and rivers, and dozens of waterfalls, many unnamed. This remote area also contains one of the most extensive virgin hardwood forests east of the Rocky Mountains, as well as nearly every type of flora and fauna native to Michigan. The streams that feed Lake Superior host large schools of spawning salmon and steelhead trout each fall.

This rugged region of the Upper Peninsula offers both mountain challenge and Great Lakes beauty in its more than 90 miles of trails. The trail system in Porcupine Mountains Wilderness State Park allows hikers the opportunity to match skill and experience with their available time to create the perfect outdoor adventure. Trail lengths vary considerably, from the 16-mile Lake Superior Trail, which extends along the shoreline of its namesake, to the 0.75-mile Greenstone Falls Access Trail. The park visitor center can provide an updated trail map that also locates camping possibilities in the park, designed specifically to complement USGS maps.

Hikes through the Porcupine Mountains are rated moderate to difficult, leaning toward the high end of the scale because of rugged and often remote terrain. This is not an area for the casual hiker; inexperienced hikers are cautioned to solicit the assistance of experienced hikers or, as one local hiker advised, "Take it in small bites!" Good, solid footwear is a must if you plan to venture far beyond the parking lot. The trails themselves are not easily traversed in many areas because of uneven, rocky terrain that is "booby-trapped" with roots from trailside trees and stretches of coarse sand. Be prepared for all conditions, and do not take the region lightly.

Elevations in the Porcupines range from the sublime shoreline of Lake Superior to severe heights as hikers climb 1,958-foot Summit Peak. The most prominent site in the park is the Lake of the Clouds Overlook, offering easy access and a stunning view of the park's rugged interior. A second, less accessible overlook is the Summit Peak Tower, which looks out at the scenic Superior shoreline.

Throughout the park, remnants of a once-active copper industry can be found, marked by a few posts and beams. More than three dozen mines are scattered throughout the park; hikers should be aware of the potential hazards these areas pose. The park's wilderness is framed by towering pines, hundreds of years old, which escaped the saw. Loggers were allowed into one small section of the park following a major storm, but there are few other reminders of the rich logging history of northern Michigan within park confines.

The park is generally free of snow and ice from May through October, but the prime season to visit the park is during fall, when the Porcupine Mountains are colored by the season. The park is used by deer and small game hunters, so hikers are cautioned to wear bright clothing in the park after September 15. Visiting the park immediately after the snow and ice have melted can be an especially quiet time in this vast wilderness—and cold, too. Waiting until the weather warms, however, will expose hikers to squadrons of flying, biting insects, such as blackflies, no-see-ums, mosquitoes, deerflies, and gnats.

Trailheads for many of the park's twenty-two trails are located at junctions with other pathways through the interior region of this wilderness area, creating a web of possible loops. Each trail described in this book is treated separately rather than as part of a complete loop; the trail descriptions include notations on intersections and junctions with other pathways in the Porcupines. This approach is meant to give hikers more flexibility in planning a trip in the region. Putting together a hike to match hikers' abilities and timetables should require little more skill than it takes to assemble a peanut butter sandwich.

To reach the park, head to the western Upper Peninsula. The east end of the park is 10 miles north of Bergland on Michigan Highway 64 and 14 miles from Ontonagon along the shores of Lake Superior on Michigan Highway 107. The west entrance to the park is 16 miles from Wakefield, on County Road 519.

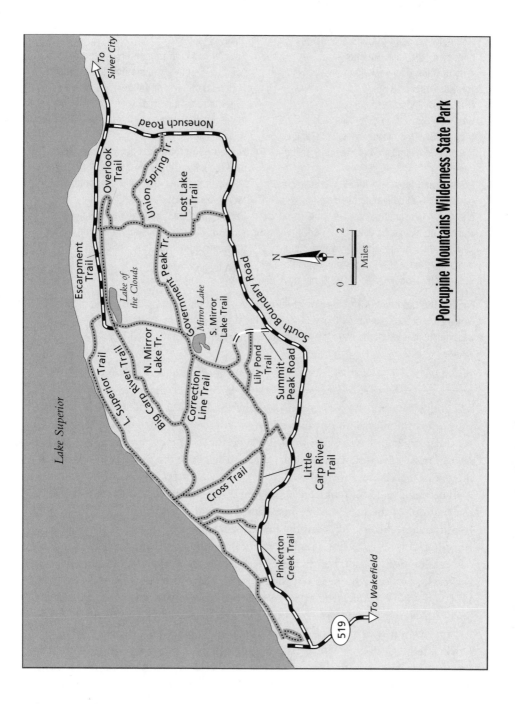

Porcupine Mountains Wilderness State Park

9 Lake Superior Trail

Highlights: A point-to-point hike across the park along the Lake Superior shoreline.

Type of hike: Backpack linear hike.

Total distance: 16 miles.

Difficulty: Moderate to difficult.

Best months: July through October.

Maps: USGS Thomaston, White Pine, and Carp River; updated trail map at the park's visitor center.

Permits and fees: As with all Michigan state parks, a $4.00 daily motor vehicle fee is charged. A seasonal pass is available for $20. There is no charge for use of the park's rustic cabins, which are reserved on a first-come, first-served basis. Campsites are available in the park: modern sites, $19.00 per day; rustic sites, $9.00.

Special considerations: This is a point-to-point hike; unless you pre-position a second vehicle at the end of the trek, you have to either retrace your steps or make arrangements for someone to transport you back to your vehicle.

For more information: Park Manager, Porcupine Mountains Wilderness State Park, 599 Michigan Highway 107 (M-107), Ontonagon, MI 49953; (906) 885-5275.

Parking and trailhead facilities: Parking is plentiful at either trailhead; other than water, no services are available.

(See map on page 45.)

Finding the trailhead: Hikers starting at the eastern end of the trail start 1 mile east of the parking lot for the Lake of the Clouds Overlook. The trailhead is on the north side of M-107. The west trailhead is at the Presque Isle Campground at the end of County Road 519.

The hike:

The longest trail in the park, the Lake Superior Trail is a point-to-point trail that runs nearly the full width of this wilderness area. The most practical route for hikers along this trail that shadows the Lake Superior shoreline is to hike into the sunset, east to west. That way, once you have descended from the Escarpment Overlook, the rest of the hike is downhill.

The first 2 miles of trail from the trailhead off M–107 head generally north to the "bottom of the hill" and the first approach to the shoreline of Lake Superior. Near the shore, hikers will reach the first man-made shelter along this 16-mile trail, Buckshot Cabin, just a few hundred yards ahead after you hit the bottom of the descent. It is nearly 7 miles to the next shelter (other than one you can carry in your backpack), so those who need rest should pause here.

For the next 3 miles, the trail plays hide-and-seek with the shoreline of Lake Superior, often screened from sight but loud with the sound of pounding waves. The first marked junction in the trail comes next, showing the way to a spot called Lone Rock, a huge glacial remnant. This is a good spot to set up a tent and allow those knees to recover from the earlier descent to the lakeshore. About 1 mile farther down the trail, hikers will find an Adirondack shelter. Hikers looking for a roof over

A campsite with a view: Lake of the Clouds provides the backdrop for the beauty of the trail system in the Porcupine Mountains Wilderness State Park.

their heads might want to check in here, since this will be the last such shelter for nearly 3 miles.

From the shelter it's an easy hike to the mouth of the Big Carp River and the first junction with another major trail on the east bank, the Big Carp River Trail (see Hike 10). Past the junction, a short wooden bridge provides access to the west bank of the river. Once across the bridge, hikers will find the posted junction with the next trail, the Cross Trail (Hike 16). Just a stone's throw from the junction is the Big Carp River Cabin. If hikers follow the set of steps to the campground named after the nearby river, a second cabin, the Lake Superior Cabin, is just a few short yards away. A possible side trip from this point would be an easy 1-mile hike to Shining Cloud Falls, the highest waterfall in the park.

About 0.5 mile west of the campground, a bridge provides access over Toledo Creek. About 1 mile farther is the next major junction, the northern start point for the Little Carp River Trail. Hikers will find a prepared campsite on the east bank of the river. Crossing the river, you reach the west bank and a short spur trail to the Little Carp River Cabin "climbing about a million stairs!" Here also is the next trail junction, the northern trailhead for the Pinkerton Creek Trail (Hike 15).

After passing the junction, hikers will find it is a quick 0.5 mile to Pinkerton Creek. The creek crossing is made tough by a 60-foot-deep ravine guarding the flanks of the waterway. You are only about 6 miles from the end of the Lake Superior Trail but face some of the toughest terrain found anywhere along its length. Still, if it's scenery you want, this is the place to be. Before the trail's end, you'll cross three small creeks without the aid of bridges; rock-hoppers will be able to keep their boots dry.

Hikers will reach a junction with a short spur trail leading to Speakers Cabin, which is nearly 0.5 mile from the main trail. At the junction, hikers have about 2 miles left on the Lake Superior Trail. The terrain separating hikers from here to the Presque Isle Campground is rocky and punctuated by ravines. The final barrier, the Presque Isle River, is Michigan's premier white-water river, but bridges and board-walks will make the crossing a dry one.

On the east bank of the river, hikers will pass the junction with the East River Trail, one-half of the loop trail that flanks the Presque Isle River and provides campers a chance to "get lost" in the wilderness of the mountains (see Additional Hikes). A steep descent to a swing bridge over the river, a steep climb to the top of the ravine carved by the waterway, a pause to take in the beauty of the last landmark on the Lake Superior Trail, and—it's over!

Key points:

2.0 Buckshot Cabin

5.0 Lone Rock (campsite)

6.0 Adirondack shelter

9.0 Big Carp River Cabin

10.7 Little Carp River Cabin

13.5 Speakers Cabin

10 Little and Big Carp River Trails

Highlights: Short trails that shadow two of the park's best fishing rivers. Scenic hikes offering waterfalls, upland habitats, and Great Lakes shoreline vistas.

Type of hike: Backpack loop hikes.

Total distance: Little Carp River Trail Loop, 11 miles; Big Carp River Trail Loop, 9 miles.

Difficulty: Moderate and, at times, easy.

Best months: Late summer and fall.

Maps: USGS Thomaston, White Pine, and Carp River; updated trail map at the park's visitor center.

Permits and fees: As with all Michigan state parks, a $4.00 daily motor vehicle fee is charged. A seasonal pass is available for $20. There is no charge for use of the park's rustic cabins, which are reserved on a first-come,

first-served basis. Campsites are available in the park: modern sites, $19.00 per day; rustic sites, $9.00.

Special considerations: Footing along some stretches of the trails can be slippery. While there are a few small streams to cross, bridges span most waterways along these routes. Early-spring hikers will be plagued by swarms of mosquitoes and blackflies.

For more information: Park Manager, Porcupine Mountains Wilderness State Park, 599 Michigan Highway 107 (M-107), Ontonagon, MI 49953; (906) 885-5275.

Parking and trailhead facilities: Adequate parking is available for the Big Carp River Trail.

(See map on page 45.)

Finding the trailhead: The Little Carp River Trail is an internal trail, starting from the north end at a well-marked junction with the Lake Superior Trail and from the south end at Mirror Lake. The Big Carp River Trail starts at the end of the parking lot for the Lake of the Clouds Overlook at the end of M–107.

The hikes:

Little Carp River Trail—From the trail's junction with the Lake Superior Trail, hikers will lose elevation as they make the trek to the bed of the Little Carp River. This will be the first of many ups and downs along this trail; the route gains nearly 1,000 feet in elevation from trailhead to trailhead.

Within the next 2 miles hikers will make a number of stream crossings, all without the aid of bridges. About 0.5 mile later, the first of two waterfalls, Explorer Falls, comes into view. The next, Trapper Falls, comes several hundred yards farther down the trail. From the falls, the trail is fairly easy to negotiate and follows the trace of the river. It begins to get a bit steeper as it makes a turn northwest, heading for its terminus at Mirror Lake.

About 6 miles after leaving Lake Superior, hikers will reach the Cross Trail and a short trail that leads to the Greenstone Falls Cabin. Several hundred yards farther, hikers will meet the access trail to Little Carp River Road, to the south. The trail continues its trace toward Mirror Lake, eventually climbing to an elevation of nearly 1,600 feet before it meets up with the Lily Pond trailhead, on the south (right) side

A number of tributaries feeding Lake Superior play host to schools of salmon and steelhead trout each fall.

of the main trail. The next 3 miles are a "walk in the park," according to park officials, compared with previous trail miles. The next trail junction is found about 1
mile later, when the Little Carp route meets the Beaver Creek Trail.

Just before reaching Mirror Lake, hikers will reach the South Mirror Lake Trail
and, a few yards later, the Correction Line Trail. Continue on the Little Carp River
Trail, which ends on the northwest corner of the lake.

Big Carp River Trail—This trail runs east-west through the park from the Lake
of the Clouds Overlook to the Lake Superior Trail at the mouth of the Big Carp
River. The first 2 miles of trail carry hikers from the overlook's rugged beauty and
the height of the escarpment down into the valley of the Big Carp River. It is quite
a drop in elevation but not a difficult hike.

At the bottom, the hike through the river valley is actually quite enjoyable and
fairly easy. Nearly 4 miles along, hikers cross the river for the first time with the aid
of a footbridge and then reach a junction with the Correction Line Trail. From here,
the trail climbs out of the valley for about 1.5 miles before dropping back down so
that hikers can cross the river once again. After making the crossing, hikers climb
once again out of the river valley and into a heavily forested area for a 2-mile hike
to Shining Cloud Falls. From the falls, hikers drop back down to the river, following the trace to its rendezvous with Lake Superior.

Key points:

Little Carp River Trail:
2.5 Explorer Falls

3.0 Trapper Falls

7.0 Greenstone Falls Cabin

Big Carp River Trail:
6.0 Crossing of Big Carp River

8.0 Shining Cloud Falls

11 Government Peak Trail

Highlights: The trail shadows the Upper Carp River to provide a respite at Mirror Lake.

Type of hike: Backpack linear trail.

Total distance: 7.5 miles.

Difficulty: Moderate.

Best months: Late summer and fall.

Maps: USGS Thomaston, White Pine, and Carp River; updated trail map at the park's visitor center.

Permits and fees: As with all Michigan state parks, a $4.00 daily motor vehicle fee is charged. A seasonal pass is available for $20. There is no charge for use of the park's rustic cabins, which are reserved on a first-come, first-served basis. Campsites are available in the park: modern sites, $19.00 per day; rustic sites, $9.00.

Special considerations: Footing along some stretches of the trails can be slippery. Although there are a few small streams to cross, bridges span most waterways. Early-spring hikers will be plagued by swarms of mosquitoes and blackflies.

For more information: Park Manager, Porcupine Mountains Wilderness State Park, 599 Michigan Highway 107 (M–107), Ontonagon, MI 49953; (906) 885-5275.

Parking and trailhead facilities: Parking is limited at both trailheads.

(See map on page 45.)

Finding the trailhead: The northern trailhead is 0.5 mile east of Escarpment Overlook, on the south side of the road. The western trailhead is the junction with the North Mirror Lake Trail, about 1 mile east of the lake.

The hike:

From the north trailhead, 0.4 mile east of the parking lot for the Escarpment Overlook, hikers head south along the trail and quickly encounter three junctions with other trails. Within about 1 mile hikers pass the east end of the Escarpment Trail (Hike 17) and then both ends of the 3-mile Overlook Trail loop.

The first crossing of the Upper Carp River is next, about 1 mile from the trailhead. For the next mile, hikers shadow the river as they head for the junction with the Union Spring Trail. Within the next mile, Trap Falls comes into view before another crossing of the Upper Carp must be negotiated.

Next is a junction with another major trail, the Lost Lake Trail. From this junction, the main pathway swings west. In 2 miles hikers will reach the headwaters of the Upper Carp River, where the trail begins to steepen as it rises toward the summit of Government Peak. As quickly as it rose, the trail drops down the west side of the peak and heads off for the final 2 miles to Mirror Lake. Nearly 0.5 mile from the lake, hikers will reach the junction with the North Mirror Lake Trail and the official end of the Government Peak Trail. If you intend to finish your day on the shores of Mirror Lake, you will have to go the short distance on a portion of the North Mirror Lake Trail to do so.

Key points:

1.0 Bridge over the Upper Carp River

2.0 Trap Falls and second bridge over the Upper Carp River

3.0 Headwaters of the Upper Carp River

6.0 Mirror Lake

7.5 Junction with North Mirror Lake Trail

12 Lost Lake Trail

Highlights: A scenic trail through mature wild forest to reach Lost Lake.

Type of hike: Backpack linear hike.

Total distance: 4.5 miles.

Difficulty: Moderate.

Best months: Midsummer and fall.

Maps: USGS Thomaston, White Pine, and Carp River; updated trail map at the park's visitor center.

Permits and fees: As with all Michigan state parks, a $4.00 daily motor vehicle fee is charged. A seasonal pass is available for $20. There is no charge for use of the park's rustic cabins, which are reserved on a first-come, first-served basis. Campsites are available in the park: modern sites, $19.00 per day; rustic sites, $9.00.

Special considerations: Footing along some stretches of the trails can be slippery. Stream crossings will have to be negotiated without the use of bridges. Early-spring hikers will be plagued by swarms of mosquitoes and black-flies.

For more information: Park Manager, Porcupine Mountains Wilderness State Park, 599 Michigan Highway 107 (M–107), Ontonagon, MI 49953; (906) 885-5275.

Parking and trailhead facilities: Parking at the southern trailhead is limited.

(See map on page 45.)

Finding the trailhead: The southern trailhead is along South Boundary Road, 7 miles from the M–107 junction. The start point is across the road from the Lost Creek Outpost Campground. The northern trailhead is at the trail's junction with the Government Peak Trail.

The hike:

From the southern trailhead, the first 0.5 mile of the trail passes through a forested area but quickly climbs along a rocky pathway to the shoulder of Lost Creek. For about 1.5 miles from the trailhead, hikers begin a steady ascent to reach an elevation of just over 1,500 feet. As you reach the high point of the trail near Lost Lake, the immense conifers provide a cathedral-like setting. Take in an equally picturesque view of the lake.

The trail then passes along the southern shore of Lost Lake and then around the western edge before assuming a northern course. Hikers leaving the shoreline of the lake should be prepared for a steep descent: You lose more than 200 feet in elevation in a quick 0.5 mile. Less than 1 mile from the lake, hikers will have to wade the cold waters of the Upper Carp River. There is no bridge here, but the crossing can provide welcome relief from the hardness of the trail.

For the final 1.5 miles, hikers make a slow climb to the junction with the Government Peak Trail.

Key points:

0.5 Lost Creek

2.0 Lost Lake

2.9 Wade across Upper Carp River

4.5 Junction with Government Peak Trail

13 Correction Line Trail

Highlights: A connector trail between the Big Carp River, Mirror Lake, or the Little Carp River.

Type of hike: Connector trail.

Total distance: 3 miles.

Difficulty: Moderate.

Best months: Midsummer and late fall.

Maps: USGS Thomaston, White Pine, and Carp River; updated trail map at the park's visitor center.

Permits and fees: As with all Michigan state parks, a $4.00 daily motor vehicle fee is charged. A seasonal pass is available for $20. There is no charge for use of the park's rustic cabins, which are reserved on a first-come, first-served basis. Campsites are available in the park: modern sites, $19.00 per day; rustic sites, $9.00

Special considerations: Much of this trail is wet throughout most of the year, and footing will be soggy. Early-spring hikers will be plagued by swarms of mosquitoes and black-flies.

For more information: Park Manager, Porcupine Mountains Wilderness State Park, 599 Michigan Highway 107 (M–107), Ontonagon, MI 49953; (906) 885-5275.

Parking and trailhead facilities: No amenities other than those you carry in.

(See map on page 45.)

Finding the trailhead: The trail is another of the park's interior trails that can only be accessed from another major trail. The trailheads are (1) at the junction with the Big Carp River Trail, 4 miles from Lake Superior; and (2) at a posted junction with the North Mirror Lake Trail on the north shore of Mirror Lake, 5 miles from Lake of the Clouds.

The hike:

Begin at the west trailhead at a junction with the Big Carp River Trail, on the east shore of the Big Carp River (see Hike 10). The first 1 mile of the Correction Line Trail crosses very wet ground as the trail moves away from the river. Hikers won't leave the soggy footing behind until they cross Landlookers Creek. The area remains wet much of the year, making for an unavoidably sloppy start.

Once across the creek, hikers will make a slow ascent of nearly 2 miles. At first the climb is easy, but it quickens and does not get easier until hikers top out at a point nearly 1,600 feet high overlooking Mirror Lake. It is only a few hundred yards downhill to the lake and the end of this trail. At the final junction, the Little Carp River Trail heads west, and the North Mirror Lake Trail heads east.

Key point:

1.0 Start 2-mile ascent to Mirror Lake

14 Mirror Lake Trails

Highlights: Connector trails near Mirror Lake offering optional routes to major interior park trails.

Type of hike: Connector trail.

Total distance: North Mirror Lake Trail, 6.5 miles; South Mirror Lake Trail, 2.5 miles.

Difficulty: Easy to moderate.

Best months: Midsummer and fall.

Maps: USGS Thomaston, White Pine, and Carp River; updated trail map at the park's visitor center.

Permits and fees: As with all Michigan state parks, a $4.00 daily motor vehicle fee is charged. A seasonal pass is available for $20. There is no charge for use of the park's rustic cabins, which are reserved on a first-come,

first-served basis. Campsites are available in the park: modern sites, $19.00 per day; rustic sites, $9.00.

Special considerations: Most of these trails are wet throughout most of the year, and footing will be soggy. Early-spring hikers will be plagued by swarms of mosquitoes and black-flies.

For more information: Park Manager, Porcupine Mountains Wilderness State Park, 599 Michigan Highway 107 (M–107), Ontonagon, MI 49953; (906) 885–5275.

Parking and trailhead facilities: Parking is limited at Summit Peak Road.

(See map on page 45.)

Finding the trailhead: The North Mirror Lake Trail begins at Mirror Lake and ends at the parking lot for the Lake of the Clouds Overlook. The South Mirror Lake trailhead is at the end of Summit Peak Road, 1.5 miles from South Boundary Road.

The hikes:

North Mirror Lake Trail—From the trailhead on the north shore of Mirror Lake, the trail heads north toward Lake of the Clouds, 4 miles away. The first mile is considered easy, but it also requires that hikers cross a moderate number of small streams before reaching a junction with the Government Peak Trail.

From the junction, the next 2.5 miles of trail are a series of gentle climbs and steep drops to the ridges overlooking Lake of the Clouds. The long drop to the bottom of a ridge to cross Scott Creek is the final marker before you reach the lake. From the western edge of the lake, the trail turns right to follow the north shore before it climbs to the parking lot for the overlook. Hikers will climb nearly 200 feet from the lake before reaching the end of the trail.

South Mirror Lake Trail—From the trailhead on Summit Peak Road, this 2.5-mile trail heads north to the western shore of Mirror Lake. The trail is easy to follow but involves a series of major ups and downs, several of them rising or falling 200 feet or more. Just over 1 mile from the trailhead, hikers will reach a junction with the Summit Peak Trail. In another mile, hikers must cross the Little Carp River to reach a junction with the Little Carp River Trail. The next junction will be with the Correction Line Trail. The final few hundred yards of the trail are along the north shore of Mirror Lake, continuing to a point where the southern trail merges into the North Mirror Lake Trail.

Key points:

North Mirror Lake Trail:

4.0 Junction with Government Peak Trail

10.5 Scott Creek crossing

13.0 South Mirror Lake Overlook

South Mirror Lake Trail (from South Boundary Road trailhead):

1.0 Summit Peak Trail junction

2.2 Little Carp River junction

2.6 Correction Line Trail junction

15 Pinkerton Creek Trail

Highlights: A brief and pleasant connector trail to or from the Little Carp River.
Type of hike: Connector trail.
Total distance: 3 miles.
Difficulty: Easy.
Best months: Midsummer and fall.
Maps: USGS Thomaston, White Pine, and Carp River; updated trail map at the park's visitor center.
Permits and fees: As with all Michigan state parks, a $4.00 daily motor vehicle fee is charged. A seasonal pass is available for $20. There is no charge for use of the park's rustic cabins, which are reserved on a first-come, first-served basis. Campsites are available in the park: modern sites, $19.00 per day; rustic sites, $9.00.
Special considerations: Hikers looking to avoid the rugged western end of the Lake Superior Trail use this as a bypass trail.
For more information: Park Manager, Porcupine Mountains Wilderness State Park, 599 Michigan Highway 107 (M–107), Ontonagon, MI 49953; (906) 885-5275.
Parking and trailhead facilities: Parking at the southern trailhead is limited.

(See map on page 45.)

Finding the trailhead: The well-marked southern trailhead is located along South Boundary Road, 20 miles west of the park's visitor center and about 5 miles east of the Presque Isle Campground. The northern trailhead is at the intersection of the Pinkerton Creek and Lake Superior Trails, 5.5 miles east of the Presque Isle River.

The hike:

From the southern trailhead, the first mile of trail leads through mature hardwood stands before it reaches its namesake, Pinkerton Creek. A wooden bridge allows for a dry-foot crossing; within a few yards, a second, smaller creek and another handy bridge have to be crossed as you hike through stands of ancient hardwoods and conifers. With less than 0.5 mile to go to the end of the trail, hikers break out on the west bank of the Little Carp River and shadow the river for the final few hundred yards to the shore of Lake Superior.

Key points:

1.0 Pinkerton Creek
2.5 Little Carp River

16 Cross Trail

Highlights: A connector trail between two of the park's major trails, the Lake Superior Trail and the Little Carp River Trail.

Type of hike: Connector trail.

Total distance: 5 miles.

Difficulty: Moderate.

Best months: September through early November.

Maps: USGS Thomaston, White Pine, and Carp River; updated trail map at the visitor center.

Permits and fees: As with all Michigan state parks, a $4.00 daily motor vehicle fee is charged. A seasonal pass is available for $20. There is no charge for use of the park's rustic cabins, which are reserved on a first-come,

first-served basis. Campsites are available in the park: modern sites, $19.00 per day; rustic sites, $9.00.

Special considerations: Most of this trail is wet throughout most of the year, and footing will be soggy. Early-spring hikers will be plagued by swarms of mosquitoes and blackflies.

For more information: Park Manager, Porcupine Mountains Wilderness State Park, 599 Michigan Highway 107 (M–107), Ontonagon, MI 49953; (906) 885-5275.

Parking and trailhead facilities: Parking is limited at the alternative southern trailhead.

(See map on page 45.)

Finding the trailhead: The southern trailhead is at the junction with the Little Carp River Trail, 5.5 miles south of the Lake Superior shoreline and west of Greenstone Falls, on the north bank of the Little Carp River. Another southern entry to the trail is possible from a parking lot along South Boundary Road, near the junction with Little Carp River Road. The distance from the parking area to the trailhead is 0.5 mile. The northern trailhead is at a junction with the Lake Superior Trail at the mouth of the Big Carp River.

The hike:

From the southern trailhead on the Little Carp Trail hikers go 0.5 mile before dropping into an extensive wet area known as the Memengwa Swamp. The wetlands can be especially buggy early in the hiking season and will be challenging regardless of the time of year you visit. After 1.5 trail miles, the swamp turns into a relatively dry forest as hikers begin to climb out of the wet basin. A slight climb over the next mile of trail ends at an overlook that presents the first look at the Big Carp River.

From here the trail drops quickly over a short distance, losing nearly 100 feet of elevation. Hikers are within 0.5 mile of the Lake Superior Trail as they pass Bathtub Falls, the final adjustment in elevation made by the Big Carp River as it spills toward Lake Superior. The end of the trail comes quickly. The trailhead on the Lake Superior Trail is on the west side of the river.

Key points:

0.5 Start of the Memengwa Swamp

2.0 End of Memengwa Swamp

4.5 Bathtub Falls

17 Escarpment Trail

Highlights: Spectacular scenic views of Lake of the Clouds.
Type of hike: Linear trail.
Total distance: 4 miles.
Difficulty: Moderate.
Best months: August through October.
Maps: USGS Thomaston, White Pine, and Carp River; updated trail map at the park's visitor center.
Permits and fees: As with all Michigan state parks, a $4.00 daily motor vehicle fee is charged. A seasonal pass is available for $20. There is no charge for use of the park's rustic cabins, which are reserved on a first-come, first-served basis. Campsites are available in the park: modern sites, $19.00 per day; rustic sites, $9.00.
Special considerations: Early-spring hikers will be plagued by swarms of mosquitoes and blackflies. Changes in elevation require a slow pace, even for experienced hikers.
For more information: Park Manager, Porcupine Mountains Wilderness State Park, 599 Michigan Highway 107 (M-107), Ontonagon, MI 49953; (906) 885-5275.
Parking and trailhead facilities: Plenty of parking but no amenities or services available at the trailhead.

(See map on page 45.)

Finding the trailhead: The trailhead is the same one used at the Lake of the Clouds Overlook for the North Mirror Lake Trail, but the Escarpment Trail turns southeast 0.5 mile after leaving the trailhead.

The hike:

This point-to-point trail offers a unique view of the most scenic point in the park, Lake of the Clouds. A spur trail about midway between Cloud Peak and Cuyahoga Peak divides the trail in half.

Leaving the Lake of the Clouds Overlook, hikers actually start the trek on North Mirror Lake Trail, heading south for nearly 0.5 mile before breaking away on the Escarpment Trail. From the junction, the path swings east. Hikers will start climbing as they head for the first landmark, Cloud Peak. At the peak, hikers will enjoy a look at the east end of Lake of the Clouds, something few park visitors get to enjoy. After a quick drop off the east side of the peak, hikers will reach the junction to a shortcut spur leading north back to M-107. Hikers are now at the halfway point of the trail.

Continuing east, the next landmark, the Carp Lake Mine, is reached just prior to the start of the climb to Cuyahoga Peak. The trail passes the actual summit and starts a long descent to the eastern trailhead, passing the Cuyahoga Mine about 400 yards from the junction with the Government Peak Trail.

Turn north (left) at the junction for a 300-yard hike back to M-107.

Key points:

2.0 Cloud Peak
3.0 Carp Lake Mine
3.6 Cuyahoga Mine

Honorable Mentions

Overlook Trail Loop The 3.5-mile Overlook Trail shares a trailhead with the Government Peak Trail for less than 0.5 mile. The short loop actually traces a portion of the longer Government Peak Trail to return to the parking lot on M–107. This loop is one of the few actual round-trip hikes in the park.

The first 2 miles of this day hike are easy, but hikers will then climb steadily to a point just over 1,500 feet in elevation. After the climb, the remaining 1.5 miles are downhill to the junction with the Government Peak Trail. You will lose more than 350 feet from the trail's high point before you reach the southern junction.

Once you reach the junction, turn back north (left) for the 0.7-mile hike back to the M–107 trailhead.

Whitetail Path The trailhead is located on the south side of M–107, near Union Bay Campground. This 1-mile trail is a spur trail, offering a level, easy hike used primarily by campers from Union Bay Campground. It provides access to the park's interpretive center.

Visitor Center Nature Trail The nature trail starts at the rear of the visitor center. This trail is one of two nature trails at the east end of the park. The 1-mile loop is punctuated by a number of stations describing flora of the area. It connects to the Whitetail Path for just a few yards before returning to the visitor center.

Union Mine Trail The trailhead for this 1-mile trail is approximately 2 miles south of the park's headquarters and the M–107 junction on South Boundary Road. Signposts along this interpretive route permit hikers a choice of directions as the trail shadows the Union and Little Union Rivers. It is a brief, miniature view of the interior of the park, revealing a glimpse into the past of the region's mining activity.

Union Spring Trail The eastern trailhead for this trail is several hundred yards south of the Union Mine trailhead; the western end of the trail is the junction with Government Peak Trail, 4 miles away. This easy, nearly level trail offers an alternative way to reach the Government Peak Trail, bypassing the more rugged start on the trek to Mirror Lake.

Leaving the trailhead off South Boundary Road, hikers move along an ancient two-track for nearly 0.6 mile. A gate blocks potential vehicular access; beyond that point, the trail heads west into the heart of the park. The trail crosses the Union River, heading west, and Union Spring. A somewhat confusing junction appears next, and park officials warn hikers to be ready for it. About 1 mile from the trailhead, the trail and a grown-over two-track come together. The trail heads west and the roadway turns off to the northwest.

The wilderness nature of the "Porkies" make this park a popular destination.

Several hundred yards from this junction, Union Spring appears—the halfway mark in the trail. The trail's remaining 2 miles continue west through a marshy area and then go up a bit to dry out for the final mile to the junction with the Government Peak Trail.

At trail's end, hikers have three choices: Do an about-face and retrace their steps to the starting point; turn right and head for M–107, about 2 miles north; or turn left and continue on the Government Peak Trail.

Summit Peak Tower Trail The trailhead for this short trail is located at the end of the parking lot at the end of Summit Peak Road. The 800 yards from the trailhead to the tower and platform atop Summit Peak are an easy hike and offer a chance to view the park's interior. The trail is easy to follow, and the ascent to the summit is not difficult. If you want to continue on this trail and link up with the South Mirror Lake Trail, be aware that the remaining 0.5 mile of the trail is not going to be easy. The steep descent down the north side of the peak prompts most visitors to simply retrace their steps to Summit Peak Road.

Beaver Creek Trail The starting point for this 2-mile trail is the same as for the Summit Peak Tower Trail, but this trail swings west out of the parking lot. This trail is another of the short access trails used to reach the Little Carp River Trail. From the trailhead at the end of Summit Peak Road, it is a quick mile to the trail's junction with the Little Carp, an easy path into the interior of the park with no major obstacles along the way.

Lily Pond Trail The eastern trailhead for the 3-mile Lily Pond Trail is found approximately 0.75 mile up Summit Peak Road from its junction with South Boundary Road. The western end of the trail is 3 miles away, at the trail's junction with the Little Carp River Trail. From the trailhead on Summit Peak Road, hikers will make a gentle climb to the high point on the trail, at just over 1,700 feet elevation.

Greenstone Falls Access Trail Hikers will find the trailhead for this 0.75-mile trail at the end of Little Carp River Road, 16 miles from the visitor center. The trail follows the Little Carp River until reaching a designated crossing point near the end of the 1,000-yard trail. Once across the river, hikers make an easy climb to the opposite shoulder and the junction with the Little Carp River Trail.

East and West River Loop The trailheads for the two trails that make up this loop are both located at the eastern edge of the Presque Isle Campground Day-Use Area. The trails form a 2-mile loop along the flanks of the Presque Isle River, a waterway considered to be the premier white-water stream in the state. Hikers descend along the gorge created by the river to cross a swing bridge before climbing back out to reach the actual start of the East River Trail. Turning south, hikers will next encounter two major waterfalls—the Manabezho and the Manido—within the first

0.5 mile of trail. Several hundred yards ahead, the final waterfall, the Nawadaha, sig-nals the final steps of the trail. Hikers will end the East River Trail on South Bound-ary Road, on the east end of the bridge.

A quick few steps across the bridge, and hikers will step onto the West River Trail, the second half of the trek, and go along the Presque Isle River. This half of the loop is easier to negotiate than the first mile and retraces many of the same sights seen earlier, including the three major waterfalls. As quickly as it began, the hike is completed as hikers climb out to the trailhead in Presque Isle Campground.

Sylvania Wilderness and Recreation Area

This large natural area comes complete with old-growth forest and pristine lakes, providing habitat for all sorts of plants and creatures. Wildflowers of all sorts, even rare orchids, can be found throughout the area. Migrating waterfowl, loons, eagles, and osprey are common sights around many of the lakes in the tract. Deer, bear, and several species of birds inhabit the area, while trophy-class smallmouth bass abound in many of the lakes along with walleye, northern pike, and panfish.

The area was purchased in 1895 by a Wisconsin-based lumber man who intended to cut its ancient red and white pines but changed his mind once he saw the area around Clark Lake. Friends joined him in preserving the beauty of the Sylvania tract and formed the Sylvania Club, and fishing and hunting replaced the activities of ax and saw. In 1967 the USDA Forest Service purchased the land and opened it to the public. In 1987 the Sylvania tract was designated a federal wilderness area, following passage of the Michigan Wilderness Act.

The wilderness area offers pristine beauty along with solitude—and a quiet ensured by a ban on motorized boats and vehicles. Designated campsites help keep the area as it was at the turn of the twentieth century. Special regulations control the use of the area and fishing within it, but the extra efforts they require pale by comparison with the wilderness they preserve.

Only the 7-mile loop around Clark Lake is a true loop trail, but spur trails can be used to create a walk through the wilderness that will take hikers deep into the nearly 19,000 acres of tangles and watery wonderland that make up this area. Many of these trails once were two-track roads into private cabin sites. Of all the campsites around the thirty-six lakes in the area, only about half can be reached via the trail systems. The remainder require a canoe to reach.

Regardless of which trail system you choose to explore, it becomes evident very quickly as to why favorite trails—and campsites—are nearest to the lakeshore: mosquitoes. The area's inland trails are tough to enjoy in late May and early June because of the presence of these needle-nosed pests and their bloodsucking colleagues, blackflies.

Special Notes: Between May 15 and September 30, every overnight camper needs to have a validated overnight camping permit, and day users must have a day use permit. Assignments of campsites will be done on a first-come, first-served basis. Camping reservations must be made with the Sylvania Visitor Center at least fourteen days in advance. Day use permits, obtained at the entrance station, cannot be reserved.

Wilderness users can make reservations by mail; these are accepted starting on January 15 of each year. To reserve a spot, campers must mail an application along with a $5.00 nonrefundable fee per reservation to the Sylvania Visitor Center, P.O. Box 276, Watersmeet, MI 49969. Starting February 1, telephone reservations may be made by calling (906) 358–4724 or (906) 358–4834 during the following times: February 1–May 14, 7:30 A.M. to 4:00 P.M. Monday through Friday; May 15– September 30, 9:00 A.M. to 5:00 P.M. seven days a week. If you are given a campsite reservation by phone, your $5.00 reservation fee must reach the center within seven days for confirmation.

The permit you receive must be validated at the park entrance when you arrive, before you hit the trail. No checkout is required, but you are asked to vacate your campsite by 2:00 P.M. on the day the permit expires. A complete packet of information, including special regulations regarding use of the area and the restrictive fishing rules will be sent along with your permit.

Use permits are not required at any other time of the year, but hikers must self-register at visitor stations in the park. Special fishing restrictions govern size and possession limits, so be sure to check before keeping any fish.

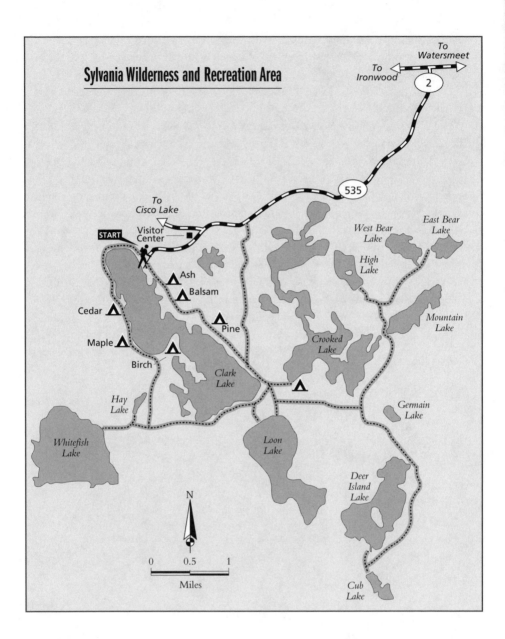

Sylvania Wilderness and Recreation Area

START

To
Cisco Lake

Visitor
Center

Ash

Balsam

Cedar

Pine

Maple

Birch

Hay
Lake

Clark
Lake

Whitefish
Lake

Loon
Lake

Crooked
Lake

West Bear
Lake

East Bear
Lake

High
Lake

Mountain
Lake

Germain
Lake

Deer
Island
Lake

Cub
Lake

To
Ironwood

To
Watersmeet

2

535

N

0   0.5   1

Miles

18 Sylvania Wilderness and Recreation Trails

Highlights: The Sylvania Wilderness and Recreation Area is an 18,327-acre step back into a quieter time in the western Upper Peninsula. The area contains old-growth forest and teems with wildlife. Twenty miles of trails connect most of the thirty-six named lakes like dots in a puzzle.

Type of hike: Backpack linear/loop hike.

Total distance: 20 miles.

Difficulty: Easy to moderate.

Best months: July through September.

Maps: Maps are available from the information centers operated by the USDA Forest Service.

Permits and fees: Daytime visitors will be charged a $5.00-per-vehicle daily use fee from May through September 30; $20 for an annual pass. Between May 15 and September 30, an overnight camping permit of $10 per day is also charged.

Special considerations: The entrance station is open 8:00 A.M. through 5:00 P.M. Saturday through Thursday and 8:00 A.M. through 6:00 P.M. on Friday. Campsite reservations may be made by phone from February 1 through May 12 only by calling the Watersmeet Visitor Center at (906) 358-4724.

For more information: Sylvania Wilderness Visitor Center, P.O. Box 276, Watersmeet, MI 49969; (906) 358-4724; Watersmeet Ranger Station, Watersmeet, MI 49969; (906) 358-4551; Gogebic Area Convention and Visitor Bureau, 126 West Arch, Ironwood, MI 49938; (906) 932-4850.

Parking and trailhead facilities: There is adequate parking at the trailhead; services in the area are limited.

Finding the trailhead: The Clark Lake trailhead is the best starting point for the trail system in the Sylvania Wilderness Area. It is located near the shore of Clark Lake at the end of the parking lot for the boat launch. Signs from the visitor center off County Road 535 will direct you to the site.

The hikes:

The 7-mile loop around Clark Lake starts just off the parking lot, about 1 mile from the visitor center. If getting away from it all is one of the reasons you hike in the first place, take the trail to the northwest (left) as you are standing at the lakeshore. Going in this direction will require a 1.5-mile hike to the first campsite, Cedar. The trail is even and easy, and by the time you reach the camp you will be on the opposite shore of Clark Lake. There are three campsites on the western shore: Maple is about 0.5 mile from Cedar, and Birch is nearly 0.75 mile from Maple, tucked in a protected little bay near the southern end of the lake.

From the Birch campsite, the trail swings directly south and into the bugs, away from the open shoreline for nearly 1 mile. About halfway along this section of trail, hikers will cross the portage between Glimmerglass and Hay Lakes. (*Portage,* by the way, is a French word meaning pick up all your stuff and carry it for a bit.) Along this

The Sylvania Wilderness and Recreation Area is an 18,327-acre step back into a quieter time in the western Upper Peninsula.

mile-long trek south, it is recommended that you either wear a head net or be prepared to put on plenty of bug repellent, especially in late spring and early summer.

At the junction with the west-east trail running from Whitefish Lake to the southern shoreline of Clark Lake, hikers can either turn west for a 0.5-mile hike to Whitefish Lake or head east for 1.5 miles toward the southern shore of Clark Lake. There are no campsites along this southern leg of the trail. Before reaching the end of the leg, hikers have several options for more diversity. One option: About 1 mile from the junction, the portage to the very popular fishing lake called Loon Lake crosses the trail. It is only about 400 yards to this excellent smallmouth bass lake. To camp here, hikers will need to portage a canoe; the campsites are all reached by water.

Another option: Nearly 300 yards farther east is a junction with the deepest penetrating trails in the Sylvania tract. Area managers advise hikers not to travel these routes from the west shore campsites, since they are not loops and only the shorter north trail has campsites. To access them, hike on for about 50 yards to the junction with the 0.5-mile trail to Badger campsite, and set up camp there. You can plan an outing into the interior of the Sylvania wilderness for the next day.

The southern trail into the wilderness area is approximately 3.5 miles long and will eventually lead along the eastern shores of Deer Island Lake and over the portage to rarely visited Cub Lake. The trail is an easy hike for even the casual hiker but cuts through fairly low-lying areas, which can mean bugs—lots of them in late spring and early summer. On the southeast corner of Deer Island Lake hikers will pass a junction with a cross-country ski trail. Keep to the right to finish the trek to Cub Lake.

The northern trail branches off the southern trail after the first mile from the junction with the Clark Lake Trail but swings north near Germain Lake. Since there are campsites available along this leg of the trail, hikers might want to consider a stay along this route at Crooked, Mountain, or East Bear Lake. About 1 mile past the fork in the trail, hikers can take a 0.5-mile side trip to High Lake, but keep in mind that this is not a loop; you will have to retrace your steps.

Once you have explored the interior of the Sylvania, the route around Clark Lake heads back north along the shore of the lake. From this point, an optional 2-mile trail will get you to the park access road, but you will have a 1-mile walk back to the parking lot along a busy paved road. Passing the junction with this "shortcut" back to civilization, the main trail continues along the shore of Clark Lake, reaching the first of three campsites, Pine, about 0.75 mile from the shortcut junction. The next two campsites, Balsam and Ash, are side by side about 0.75 mile beyond.

From the last of the campsites, Ash, it is only about 0.5 mile back to the start point at the launch site.

Key points:

Only the Clark Lake Trail is an actual loop trail; all other spur trails will split off this 7-mile loop around the lake. All trails are well marked with blue blazes and are wide and easy to hike.

Bay de Noc– Grand Island Trail

The Bay de Noc–Grand Island Trail traces the pathway used by Native Americans and fur traders moving wares from the shores of Lake Superior and northern Lake Michigan. Chippewa people used the route to portage canoes and supplies. The voyageurs, quick to use convenient routes to reach fur markets, kept the pathway alive. The 40 miles of trail closely shadow several rivers and lakes, including the Whitefish River, making this route one of the longest historic trails in the state.

The linear trail starts on its south end near the Lake Michigan community of Rapid River and terminates near Lake Ackerman, several miles back from the Lake Superior shoreline. To finish the trek between the lakes, hikers can follow the Au Train River to its outlet into Lake Superior.

The terrain is fairly level and stretches through conifer and hardwood stands and the rolling, almost rhythmic, small hills created by retreating glaciers. Wildflowers and wildlife are common sights. Hikers must deal with a fair number of small creek crossings, but those who fish will find more than a few willing brook trout in the several small creeks and brooks. The trail shadows the Whitefish River for nearly half the distance, offering great views of the river valley and the countryside to the west of it. Hikers will encounter a large number of sandy county roads, so a good map is essential for navigating. Footing is generally good, but be prepared to deal with watery crossings.

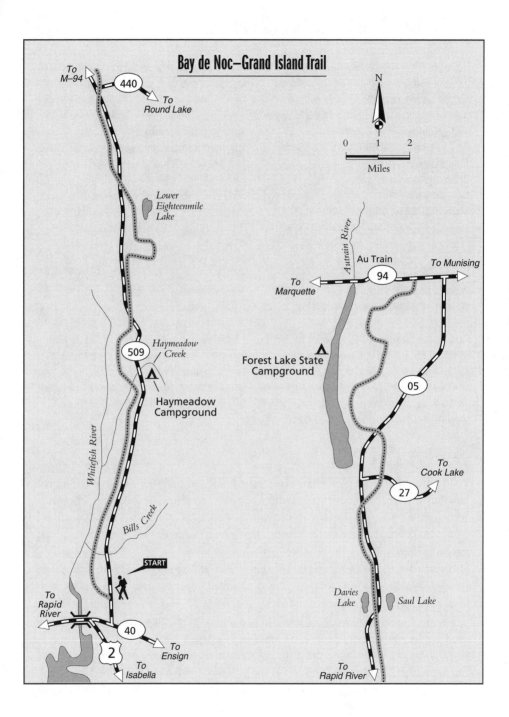

Bay de Noc–Grand Island Trail

N

0   1   2
Miles

To
M–94

440

To
Round Lake

Lower
Eighteenmile
Lake

Autrain River

Au Train

94

To Munising

To
Marquette

509

Haymeadow
Creek

Forest Lake State
Campground

Haymeadow
Campground

05

Whitefish River

Bills Creek

To
Cook Lake

27

START

To
Rapid
River

40

To
Ensign

2

To
Isabella

Davies
Lake

Saul Lake

To
Rapid River

19 Bay de Noc–Grand Island Trail

Highlights: The Bay de Noc–Grand Island Trail traces a pathway used by Native Americans and fur traders moving pelts and supplies between the shores of northern Lake Michigan and southern Lake Superior.

Type of hike: Linear trail.

Total distance: 40 miles.

Difficulty: Moderate.

Best months: Fall.

Maps: USGS Forest Lake, Lake Stella, Poplar Lake, Baker Creek, and Rapid River. The USDA Forest Service supplies an information sheet and map of the trail, but it contains only major landmarks, roads, and waterways.

Permits and fees: None.

Special considerations: Lowland areas

launch squadrons of flying, biting insects during spring and early summer. Starting September 15, hunters use the area for small and big game seasons, so wear brightly colored clothing if you visit the area after this date.

For more information: Munising Ranger District, Hiawatha National Forest, 601 Cedar Street, Munising, MI 49862; (906) 387-2512; Rapid River Ranger District, Hiawatha National Forest, 8181 U.S. Highway 2 (U.S. 2), Rapid River, MI 49878; (906) 474-6442.

Parking and trailhead facilities: There is adequate parking at each trailhead, but there are no amenities available.

Finding the trailhead: The southern trailhead near Rapid River can be reached by driving east on U.S. 2 for 2 miles to County Road 509. Turn left and drive 1.5 miles north to the parking lot and trailhead on the west side of the road. The midpoint trailhead is also on CR 509, but is 15 miles farther north, on the east side of the road. The northern trailhead can be reached by driving southwest of Munising on Michigan Highway 94. The parking lot and trailhead are on the north side of the highway, opposite Ackerman Lake.

The hike:

Following the Bay de Noc Trail is easy because of the trail care and grooming provided courtesy of the equestrians who also make good use of the route. The pathway is wide and cleared of low-lying branches to make it easier for the trail riders, which makes it doubly easy for hikers. The route is marked with blue signposts that are easily seen; turns in the trail are marked in yellow.

From the trailhead the pathway swings almost immediately north and passes through a large stand of jack pine. About 2 miles from the start, hikers make their first of many water crossings over Bills Creek. The trail shadows the Whitefish River to the west for much of the 22 miles to the midpoint trailhead, and keeps CR 509 on its right for nearly the entire 40 miles to Ackerman Lake.

Nearly 2 miles from the first water crossing, the habitat changes from conifers to hardwoods and open fields. This is also the point where having a map becomes vital, since the trail is crossed by a number of sand roads and firebreaks as well as areas of

As long as you have to cross the creek, you might as well wet a line and try to catch dinner in one of the many trout streams along the trail.

large-scale logging. About 5 miles farther north, the trail crosses Haymeadow Creek. Here hikers can end their first day on the trail at the only established campground along the trail, Haymeadow Creek Camp. To reach the campground, turn right on the first two-track past the bridge over the creek to CR 509. Then head south for 0.4 mile to the campground. You will have to retrace your steps to get back to the trail, since there is no loop to make things easier.

About 3 miles from Haymeadow Creek, the trail crosses CR 509 and stays on the east side of the road for about 5 miles as it passes through the upper end of the Whitefish River valley. Lower and Middle Eighteenmile Lakes appear east of the trail before the trail crosses CR 509 once more, staying on the other side this time for 3.5 miles.

At a junction with County Road 440, the trail switches back to the east side of CR 509 for the final 0.5 mile to the midpoint trailhead. At this point hikers leave Delta County and enter Alger County. From the midpoint trailhead, the pathway continues for 2.5 miles on the east side of CR 509 (known as H–05 in Alger County) crossing back to the west side of the road between Saul Lake to the east and Davies Lake to the west. The trail stays west of the road for 4 miles before crossing it once again, crossing County Road M–27 a mile later. About 1.5 miles farther, the trail crosses H–05 again and shoulders briefly the west shore of the Cleveland Cliffs Basin before swinging around the west shore of Lake Seventeen.

The final few miles of the trail jog left and right occasionally as the pathway winds its way to the northern trailhead at Ackerman Lake. Hikers have the option of hiking east for 10 miles along M–94 to Munising to reach the shores of Lake Superior or going 2 miles west across the Au Train River, then north on H–05 along the river, to reach the lake.

Key points:

2.0 Bills Creek

9.0 Haymeadow Creek and campground

12.0 CR 509

20.5 CR 440 junction

21.0 Midpoint trailhead

23.5 Saul Lake

28.5 M-27

30.0 Lake Seventeen

40.0 North trailhead

High Country Pathway

Veteran hikers have labeled the High Country Pathway "The Hike Assembled by Committee," since the terrain and habitat change abruptly and constantly. The complete loop takes an experienced hiker nearly seven days to complete, provided he or she doesn't make too many stops to fish or take note of the diverse flora and fauna along the trail. Wet and wild, flat and hilly are just a few of the possible combinations to be found along the 70-mile-long pathway—and that's before you include the possible combinations mentioned above.

The High Country Pathway is accessible from a good number of northern Lower Peninsula communities, depending on the start point you choose. There are also plenty of opportunities to make shorter jaunts into the heart of Pigeon River Country State Forest and the surrounding territory.

Some 1,200 elk range here, and it is not uncommon to observe white-tailed deer, wild turkeys, or black bears, along with a host of other small animals, along the trail. Eagles and ospreys soar over the region, and more than a hundred other species of birds call this area home. One of the best brook trout streams in the Midwest, the Black River, flows through the area. The Pigeon River and McMasters Creek are also good trout fisheries. Lakes encountered along the trail offer fishing for everything from rainbow trout and panfish to northern pike and bass.

20 High Country Pathway

Highlights: The varied terrain and habitats that make this hike enjoyable for hikers of all ages and experience levels also make it one of the most enjoyable wilderness-type hikes in all Michigan. The region is home to the largest free-roaming herd of Rocky Mountain elk east of the Mississippi River.

Type of hike: Backpack loop hike.

Total distance: 70 miles.

Difficulty: Easy to moderate.

Best months: Late summer and fall.

Maps: USGS Onaway, Tower, Afton, Lake Geneva, Silver Lake, Hardwood Lake, Atlanta, Hetherton, and Saunders Creek. A more convenient but less detailed pocket-sized trail description is available from the Pigeon River Country Association, P.O. Box 122, Gaylord, MI 49735.

Permits and fees: None.

Special considerations: Lowland areas launch squadrons of flying, biting insects during spring and early summer. Starting September 15, hunters use the area for small and big game seasons, so wear brightly colored clothing if you visit the area after this date.

For more information: Department of Natural Resources, Region II Headquarters, Roscommon, MI 48653; (989) 275-5151; Pigeon River Country State Forest Headquarters; (989) 983-4101; Pigeon River Country Association, P.O. Box 122, Gaylord, MI 49735.

Parking and trailhead facilities: Parking is adequate at all trailheads. Water is available at all the campgrounds except Pine Grove State Forest Campground.

Finding the trailhead: With ten state forest campgrounds and a state park, plus nearly three dozen road crossings to serve as start points for a hike along the trail, the list of possible trailheads and directions to them would fill a book. The most practical starting points are the ten campgrounds listed below:

1. **Pigeon Bridge State Forest Campground**—Sturgeon Valley Road east out of Vanderbilt for 12 miles to the campground.

2. **Elk Hill State Forest Campground**—Head east out of Vanderbilt on Sturgeon Valley Road for 15 miles to reach the campground.

3. **Pigeon River State Forest Campground**—Near the junction with Hardwood Lake Road and Sturgeon Valley Road, nearly 14 miles east of Vanderbilt.

4. **Pine Grove State Forest Campground**—Head east out of Wolverine on Webb Road for about 9 miles, and then turn south for 3 miles on Campsite Road. The trailhead is also used as a starting point for the Shingle Mill Pathway (see reference in hike description).

5. **Round Lake State Forest Campground**—Head east from Vanderbilt on Sturgeon Valley Road for about 13 miles, then south about 2 miles on Round Lake Road. The pathway is connected to the campground by a 0.5-mile spur trail to the north.

6. **Town Corner State Forest Campground**—Head north from Atlanta on M–33 for 5 miles. Turn west onto Rouse Road for 11 miles before turning north on County Road 495 to the campground. The pathway is connected to the campground by an easy 0.5-mile spur trail to the west.

7. **Jackson Lake State Forest Campground**—Drive north of Atlanta on M–33 for 7 miles, then east on County Road 624 for 0.5 mile. The pathway is reached via a 1.5-mile trail that is also part of the Clear Lake–Jackson Lake Pathway.

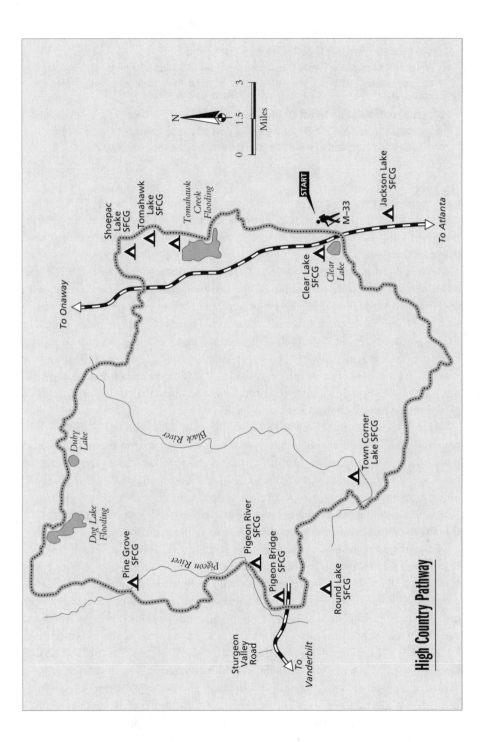

High Country Pathway

8. Clear Lake State Park—The park is 9 miles north of Atlanta on M–33. The pathway is reached via a 0.75-mile trail east of the park across M–33.

9. Tomahawk Lake State Forest Campground—Reached by driving 3 miles east on Tomahawk Lake Highway, off M–33. The pathway passes along the eastern edge of the campground.

10. Shoepac Lake State Forest Campground—Head south from Onaway on M–33 for 8 miles, then turn east on CR 634 for the 3-mile drive to the campground. A 0.25-mile trail connects the campground to the pathway and the nearby Sinkhole Pathway.

The hikes:

The High Country Pathway has as many start points as it does access points, but the trail from Clear Lake State Park, on the eastern edge of the system, described here, is one of the best.

Hikers will use the first leg of the **Clear Lake Nature Trail** to reach the start point, about 1 mile from the trailhead. The two trails merge at a gravel pit located a few hundred yards east of M–33. From here, the pathway swings north toward its first major natural landmark, Tomahawk Creek Flooding, some 9 miles away. The first section of trail passes through gentle terrain that was once the hub of activity for the region's logging industry at the turn of the century. The area is the site of the north's last great forest fire, which occurred in 1939. The trail is sandy in places, making walking a bit tough, so take your time. Low sand hills studded with stands of jack pine dominate the landscape along this section.

As you approach the Tomahawk Creek Flooding, don't be afraid to vary your path and do a little exploring. A small, primitive campground at the northeast corner of the flooding is a nice spot to set up camp, especially if you are looking for quiet. Water is available here, and so is some of the most productive fishing along the entire shoreline—this can provide a tasty respite from trail fare for the patient angler. The structure along the shoreline hides cooperative bluegill, crappie, and other panfish and even the occasional largemouth bass or cruising northern pike.

From the campground, 2 miles of easy hiking bring hikers to Tomahawk Lake State Forest Campground. Farther north, in 0.75 mile, is Shoepac Lake State Forest Campground. These two campgrounds are both well developed and have all the simple pleasures—the things road-campers demand and trail hikers find a real treat. Both campgrounds, though out of the way, are popular destinations during summer and early fall. Deer hunters use these campgrounds as main camps as late as November.

North of Shoepac Lake is the trailhead for the 2.5-mile **Sinkhole Pathway Loop.** This 2,600-acre area has been closed to all motorized travel, providing a serene setting still changing beneath the surface. The underlying karst is constantly being dissolved, and the surface layer sinks to conform to these changes in the limestone bedrock. The loop trail actually is divided into two loops—a 0.75-mile loop around the first two major sinkholes and a 1.5-mile trail that not only includes the

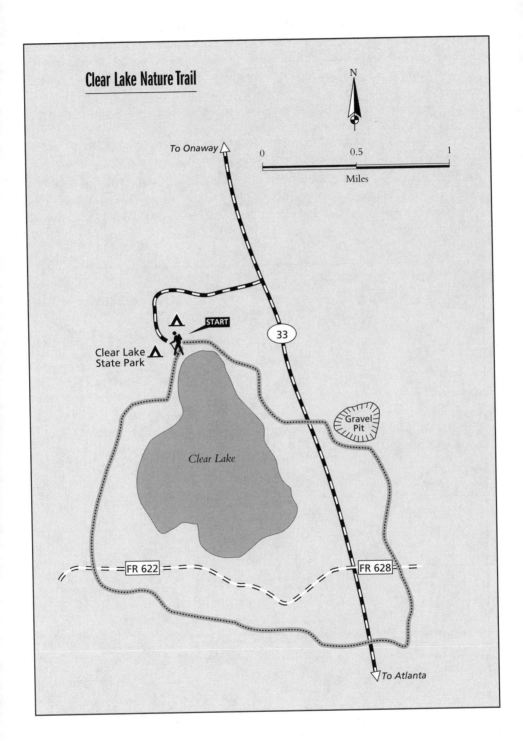

Clear Lake Nature Trail

N

To Onaway

0   0.5   1
Miles

START

Clear Lake
State Park

33

Gravel
Pit

Clear Lake

FR 622   FR 628

To Atlanta

other three major sinkholes in the region but also features a wooden stairway to the bottom of one of the deepest "sinks" in Presque Isle County. The floor of this sinkhole is more than 100 feet lower than the surface of nearby Shoepac Lake. The loops are well marked and easy to follow. Improvements made to the area include rustic fencing put up to protect the fragile slopes of the sinkholes; along the northern sections of the trails, wood chips have been used to retard plant growth that might try to reclaim the path.

The Sinkhole Pathway rejoins the High Country Pathway. The next 27 miles, from Shoepac Lake to Pine Grove State Forest Campground, is the longest stretch without a prepared or formal campground and, more important, without potable water. Hikers should carry all necessary drinking water or have the gear needed to purify water from streams and lakes along the trail. They should also be prepared for primitive camping.

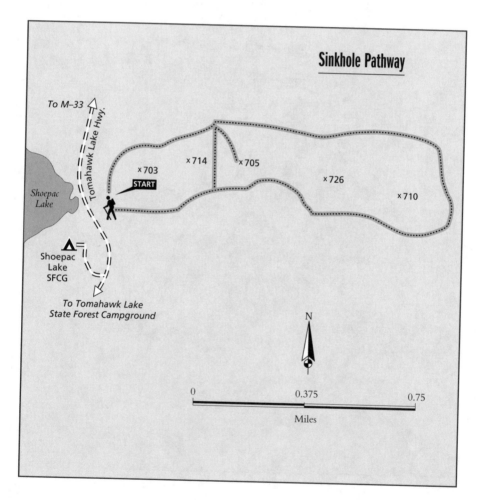

Birdlife abounds throughout the region bounded by the High Country Pathway, including large flocks of eastern wild turkeys.

From the Sinkhole Pathway, the main trail takes a decided westward bent along the fringe of a popular lake-pocked area that can be quite "moist" in the spring and after heavy rainfalls. The trail usually poses no problem for even the casual hiker, but its condition can change dramatically with added moisture.

Once across M–33, the trail crosses a good number of small streams, including Canada Creek, which merits prospecting for native brook trout. Hikers will cross into Cheboygan County 1 mile after crossing Canada Creek. The terrain rises and falls rather significantly along this 2-mile stretch of the trail, with hills rising several hundred feet then falling into marshy pockets.

The next major water obstacle, the trout-rich Black River, is preceded by another significant rise. These high areas provide an excellent spot to set up camp, since they get up out of the bug-infested lowlands. Plus, the nearby Black River serves up some of the very best brook trout fishing found anywhere in the Midwest. The water appears to be crystal-clear, but treat it before drinking or cooking with it.

About 2 miles farther west the trail drops back into the marshy wetlands surrounding Duby Lake. The swamps around the lake are alive with wildlife and, in the spring, squadrons of mosquitoes and blackflies. The lake is a picturesque 400-yard hike off the pathway, but avoid it during bug season unless you intend your visit to be a brief one. A short 400 yards farther west on the trail, hikers will find the marker pointing the way to McLavery Lake. This beautiful, remote lake is framed by white birch and delivers a view well worth the 0.5-mile hike to reach it.

Back on the main trail, the next 3.5 miles go through some of the finest mosquito habitat found anywhere in Michigan. Be prepared to use plenty of bug dope. The trail through this stretch is rated easy, but it can be damp during early spring.

Dog Lake Flooding is the next landmark to the south, about 250 yards from the trail. The lake contains a few fish, but even local fishermen won't attempt crossing its boggy shoreline until winter has solidified things. The flooding attracts large numbers of waterfowl and other wildlife, including osprey and an occasional bald eagle.

The High Country Pathway turns to the south 1.5 miles from Dog Lake Flooding and takes on a new face as well as a new direction. The wetlands and swamps are replaced by hardwood stands and dry ridgelines. The "downhill" run in a 7-mile hike through a mix of upland habitats eventually leads to the banks of the Pigeon River. At the end of this segment of the Pathway, hikers will find the remote Pine Grove State Forest Campground. This site may not be as cozy as the local Holiday Inn, but it is a welcome break from rustic camping along the more isolated northern shoulders of the trail. Toilets and drinking water are available, along with prepared tent sites that make setting up camp easier. The campground is on the east bank of the Pigeon River, a favorite hot spot for local trout fishermen throughout spring and early summer. This site is back from the normal flow of traffic, so midweek hikers will find that they have the area pretty much to themselves.

Heading south from Pine Grove, the trail weaves through stands of large maples, beeches, and even oaks. About 4 miles from Pine Grove, it merges with the first loop of the Shingle Mill Pathway. Here, the trail swings east for 2 miles until the combined trails reach the banks of the Pigeon River once again. The combined pathways shadow the river for 1.5 miles before entering the Pigeon River State Forest Campground. A second campground, the Pigeon Bridge State Forest Campground, is just 2 miles farther south, should the first campground be too crowded.

A must-stop for all hikers on the High Country Pathway is the Pigeon River Country State Forest Headquarters, located 1 mile south of the Pigeon River campground. The remaining buildings in the complex were built by the Civilian Conservation Corps in the early 1930s, from logs cut in the surrounding forest. Locally cut red and white pine logs were used to construct all the buildings in use today, including the staff house, which served as the first conservation school in Michigan.

Hikers who want to explore the loops of the **Shingle Mill Pathway** should be prepared to stay a few days, since there are 18 miles of path to check out. Loops in the pathway range from 0.75 to 11 miles long. The five loops accommodate hikers of all experience levels, even though the distance of the outer loops has given rise to a moderate classification for the trails.

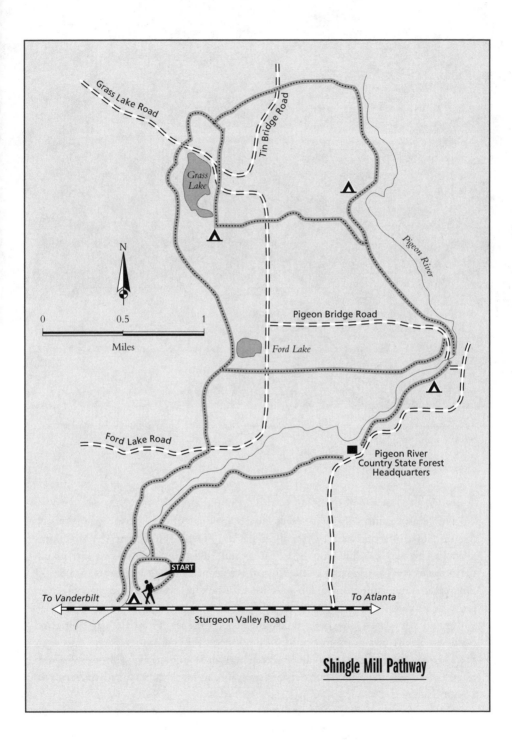

Shingle Mill Pathway

One of the Midwest's best brook trout streams, the Black River, tracks through the heart of the High Country Pathway.

The High Country Pathway traces the eastern edge of the Shingle Mill Pathway for 6.5 miles until the combined trails end at the Pigeon River State Forest Campground. The two shortest loops—0.75 mile and 1.25 miles—make easy day hikes; they parallel the eastern bank of the Pigeon River for half their lengths before dropping back to the campground. A 6-mile loop follows the course of the Pigeon River for 2 miles before turning east on a cross-country trek to join the High Country Pathway at the headquarters complex mentioned earlier. From here it continues north for 1 mile to a point just north of the Pigeon River Campground. Cross over the Pigeon River using the road bridge. The trail swings nearly due west for 1.5 miles before turning back south, meandering off and on the western banks of the Pigeon River.

A 10-mile loop follows the same trace as the 6-mile loop but continues north from the point where the shorter loop swings west. The trail shares the same route as the High Country Pathway for nearly 1.5 miles before turning west for 1 mile to reach a campsite at the southern end of Grass Lake. From the campsite, the trail heads north for 0.5 mile before turning south for the 3-mile hike back to the start point. This loop joins the southbound leg of the 6-mile loop just south of Ford Lake.

The longest loop, the 11-mile trail, picks up where the 10-mile trail turns west, continuing north for slightly more than 0.5 mile to reach the Cornwall campsite. The trail mirrors the High Country Pathway for 2 miles before turning south to blend with the southbound leg of the 10- and 6-mile Shingle Mill loops.

Hikers rejoining the High Country Pathway pick up the trail from the Pigeon Bridge State Forest Campground. Here the trail begins its eastern swing across the bottom of the trail system, cutting through rolling terrain dominated at first by impressive red pines and later by a mix of jack pine, aspen, and other second-growth stands of timber. The first trail marker is for a spur trail leading south to Round Lake State Forest Campground. The signpost is only 0.5 mile from the campground you just left. The short, easy hike to this campground puts the hiker into a setting of tall red pines and a lake filled with rainbow trout courtesy of the Department of Natural Resources. Cold, clear drinking water is available at the site.

The next 9 miles of trail are a walk back through the history of commercial logging in the region. Trail users pass through hundreds of acres of second-growth forest fostered by the industry that took millions of board feet of lumber to metropolitan markets. Be sure to keep a lookout for the remains of the Black River Overlook Tower, just west of Walled Lake. The tower was just one of many scattered throughout the region; fire watch stations have now been replaced by aircraft flying patrols over the area.

Just 1 mile farther you will find the marker for Town Corner State Forest Campground. The campground is an easy 0.5-mile hike east off the Pathway, offering good water, toilets, and a chance to swim in the warm waters of Town Corner Lake. Fishermen will find the resident largemouth bass population a challenge.

Elk sightings are fairly common over the next 10 miles. Loggers leveled the region under the "whole trees" concept, hauling away logs and truckloads of chips, leaving the entire area open to natural reforestation. The attraction for the elk is obvious: The young aspen provide a standing smorgasbord of the elk's favorite food. Deer and upland birds are also fairly common in this area.

The trail blends with the southwest corner of the Clear Lake Nature Trail for the final 2 miles back to the state park and the trailhead. The Clear Lake Nature Trail is a 5-mile loop around Clear Lake, the eastern and southern lengths of which are shared with the traces of the High Country Pathway. The trailhead, mentioned earlier in the hike description, is located in the parking lot between the two Clear Lake campgrounds in the state park. The sections of the trail that are shared by the Pathway are more than 1 mile from the nearest services in the park. So make certain you take along plenty of water and a day pack with necessary items, such as a first-aid kit.

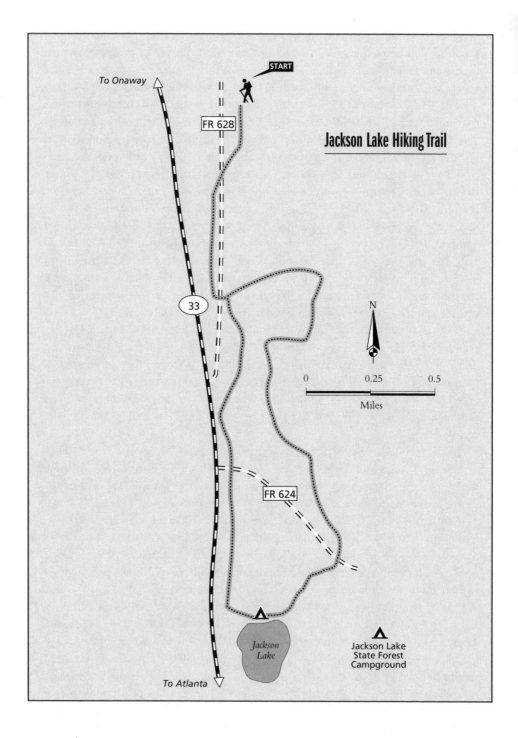

START

To Onaway

FR 628

Jackson Lake Hiking Trail

33

N

| 0 | 0.25 | 0.5 |

Miles

FR 624

Jackson
Lake

Jackson Lake
State Forest
Campground

To Atlanta

At the southeast corner of the Clear Lake Nature Trail, about 2 miles from the trailhead, is the junction with the **Jackson Lake Hiking Trail.** The trail continues to the west from this point for 1 mile before swinging back to the north at the Clear Lake Day Use Area. Water and toilets are available here. The Jackson Lake Hiking Trail heads due south from its junction with the Clear Lake Trail, along the west side of M–33 for about 3 miles to the Jackson Lake State Forest Campground. The return loop back to the junction with the Clear Lake Trail is a meandering 4.5 miles through hilly and wooded terrain dominated by a mix of large hardwoods and pines.

Key points:

1.0 Junction of Clear Lake Nature Trail and the Pathway

10.0 Tomahawk Creek Flooding and north shore campground

12.75 Shoepac State Forest Campground

13.0 Sinkhole Pathway trailhead

40.0 Pine Grove State Forest Campground

44.0 Trailhead for Shingle Mill Pathway

47.5 Pigeon River State Forest Campground

49.5 Pigeon Bridge State Forest Campground

50.5 Headquarters, Pigeon River State Forest

52.0 Round Lake State Forest Campground

62.0 Town Corner State Forest Campground

70.0 Clear Lake State Park

Shore-to-Shore Trail

The Shore-to-Shore Trail was the idea of trail riders looking for a lengthy horseback trek from shore to shore across the northern tip of Michigan's Lower Peninsula. With the help of Michigan Senator William Milliken, the trail was established in 1962. The 220-mile trail connects the town of Empire, on Lake Michigan, with the Lake Huron community of Oscoda. Hikers need to be aware of the use of the trail by equestrians, but the trail is open for all users but bicyclists. It is the longest continuous trail in the Lower Peninsula.

The trail offers a look into rural Michigan, and although it doesn't trace a path through the wilds like the North Country Trail does, it follows many northern back roads and river valleys. The Shore-to-Shore Trail is easy to hike as it follows roads and well-marked pathways through stands of conifers and hardwoods, making its way across the northern tip of the state. A group of equestrians called The Michigan Trail Riders provides a complete set of maps, as well as a trail guide, to help hikers cross the state by this route.

Although the trail is fairly "urban," it avoids the tourist destinations of Michigan's north country. Its scenery—some of the most beautiful the state offers—ranks highest on the list of special attractions. Another attraction is the Kirtland warbler habitat near Grayling and the banks of the Au Sable River, through which hikers pass. The rare Kirtland warbler is carefully watched over by the Department of Natural Resources; it is a treat to see and hear. Mixed upland and lowland habitats mean that hikers will see a wide variety of birds and animals as they hike from shore to shore.

21 Shore-to-Shore Trail

Highlights: Established in 1962 as a lengthy horseback trek from Lake Michigan to Lake Huron, this is the longest continuous trail in the Lower Peninsula.

Type of hike: Backpack linear trail.

Total distance: 220 miles.

Difficulty: Moderate.

Best months: September and October.

Maps: USGS Empire, Burdickville, Platte River, Lake Ann, Grawn, Mayfield, Jack's Landing, South Boardman, Kalkaska, Leetsville, Westwood, Starvation Lake, Frederic, Lake Margrethe, Grayling, Wakeley Lake, Roscommon North, Eldorado, Luzerne, Island Lake, Mack Lake, McKinley, Goodar, Alcona Dam Pond, Hale, Loud Dam, Sid Town, Foote Site Village, and Oscoda. The Michigan Trail Riders' brochure and guidebook, with accompanying maps, are valuable in sorting out the trail on the USGS quads.

Permits and fees: None.

Special considerations: Near Roscommon, the trail shadows the center of the state's endangered Kirtland warbler range.

For more information: Michigan Trail Riders Association, 1650 Ormond Road, White Lake, MI 48383-2344; (810) 889-3624; Traverse City Chamber of Commerce, Traverse City, MI 49684; (231) 947-5075; Michigan Department of Natural Resources, Forest Management Division, P.O. Box 30452, Lansing, MI 48909; (517) 373-1275.

Parking and trailhead facilities: Parking is adequate at each end of the trail; a full range of amenities and services are available at the trailheads.

Finding the trailhead: The western trailhead in Empire is at the junction of Michigan Highways 22 and 72. The trail follows M-72 east for several miles out of town. From the east the trail begins at the junction of River Road and U.S. Highway 23. Many hikers prefer to walk the short additional distance from the shores of Lakes Michigan and Huron to fully appreciate the shore-to-shore nature of this trail.

The hike:

Going east from the Lake Michigan shoreline to the Lake Huron coast on the sunrise side, the Shore-to-Shore Trail makes use of rural roadways, two-track jeep paths, and a variety of cross-country trails that follow river valleys. Hikers on this lengthy trail may be disappointed at first to have to spend so much time along the shoulders of prepared roads, but the scenery and relative ease of the hike will erase many of those sentiments.

From the Empire trailhead, the first day on the Shore-to-Shore is a relatively easy one, an 8-mile jaunt east from Empire to Garey Lake Camp. The route follows M-72 east for 3.5 miles to an intersection with Kitlinger Road. The trail turns south on Kitlinger Road, and follows it for 1.5 miles before turning east for another 1 mile. The trail then leaves the roadway, continuing eastward for another 2.5 miles toward the first night camping area at Garey Lake Camp. If the lower campground is filled, try the overflow area on the hill to the west.

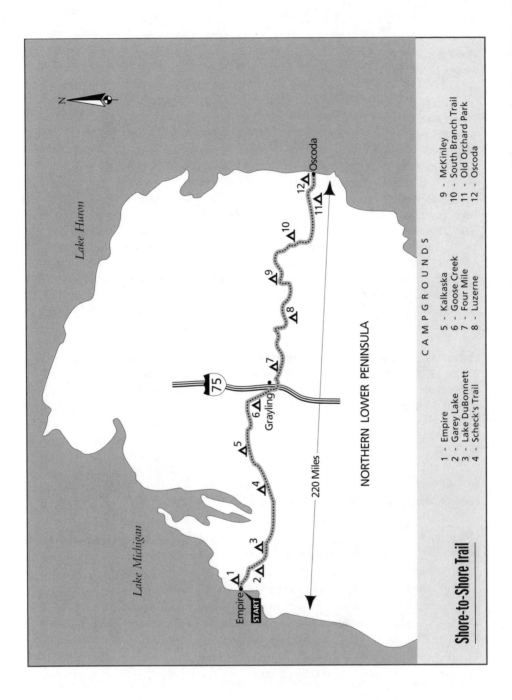

Shore-to-Shore Trail

Lake Michigan

Lake Huron

N

Empire

START

NORTHERN LOWER PENINSULA

Grayling

75

220 Miles

Oscoda

CAMPGROUNDS

1 - Empire
2 - Garey Lake
3 - Lake DuBonnett
4 - Scheck's Trail

5 - Kalkaska
6 - Goose Creek
7 - Four Mile
8 - Luzerne

9 - McKinley
10 - South Branch Trail
11 - Old Orchard Park
12 - Oscoda

The Shore-to-Shore Trail offers a peek into the scenic splendor of rural Michigan, particularly during fall's vivid displays.

Views of the surrounding countryside are worth a pause or two as you leave Garey Lake Camp. The trail heads nearly due south, crossing Pettingill Road and entering Benzie County. The path heads cross-country for the next 5.5 miles. The route then follows several small two-track roads until it reaches Oakley Road, following it east for 3.5 miles.

The trail traces Mill Road south for 1 mile before turning east again, this time onto Bronson Lake Road for the next 2.5-mile segment. It's only about 2.5 miles to the next campground, but the trail meanders north on Lake Ann Road for 0.5 mile to a small two-track on the right (east) where the trail swings east for the final 2 miles of the day. Hikers will turn onto another two-track and cross into Grand Traverse County before they reach Lake DuBonnett Camp, the second night's destination. Lake DuBonnett is also known as Mud Lake to the locals. The camp offers water and toilets and is a nice spot to break for the night.

From Lake DuBonnett, the trail follows a gravel road east for 2.4 miles to its intersection with Long Road. The trail crosses the road and heads nearly due south on another gravel road for 1.5 miles before swinging easterly for 0.5 mile; here it joins U.S. Highway 31. Hikers must follow U.S. 31 east for 0.25 mile to Grawn Road, then follow this road for 2.5 miles to Vance Road for the next 2.5-mile leg, still heading nearly due east across Grand Traverse County.

Hikers next enter the Boardman River valley, stepping off the shoulders of paved roads and onto gravel for the next 3.8 miles. At the end of this stretch of shared pathway, the trail takes a decided cross-country tack as it heads east down the river valley for the next 2.5 miles. The cross-country jaunt ends at a gravel road leading into the community of Mayfield.

The trail follows County Road 611 north for 0.5 mile before it swings east again onto Mayfield Road for about 2 miles. At this point, the trail swings northeast, heading for Scheck's Trail Camp on the banks of the Boardman River. The camp offers not only prepared sites but also all the comforts of a modern campground. It's a good place for a third night's stop.

From Scheck's Trail Camp, the trail crosses the Boardman River, heading northeasterly, and Boardman Road. It continues on gravel roads and sections of pathway for the next 3 miles. The trail next crosses Supply Road, continues northeast for 2.3 miles, then crosses Broomhead Road.

For the next 3 miles, hikers shadow North River Road but leave the roadway just after crossing into Kalkaska County. The next 5.5 miles of trail follow a series of tracks and gravel county roads as hikers head for the next campground at Kalkaska Camp, also known as Rapid River Camp. Hikers will have to cross M–72 heading north. After reaching Old Michigan Highway 72, they will follow that road southeast; it leads to the camp entrance. Kalkaska Camp offers all the comforts of a large campground. Please respect the private property along the entrance road.

Wildlife of all shapes and sizes can be seen along the trail, from the humorously waddling porcupine to the quick and graceful white-tailed deer.

Leaving the campground, hikers will head cross-country to the northeast, crossing the old Penn Central railroad tracks east of Kalkaska. Once across the tracks, hikers will enter Mayhem Swamp, also known as Kalkaska Swamp, prompting many to remember why they decided to wait until late in the bug season to attempt this hike. At the junction of Hagni and Darrach Roads, hikers will turn south for the 1-mile hike to the next junction with Myers Road.

The trail heads east from this point for 2 miles, drops south for 1 mile, then heads east first on Grass Lake Road and then takes off in an easterly trend cross-country between Grass and Bear Lakes. The cross-country trek continues for the next 4.5 miles, crossing Blue Lake Road and continuing east for another 1.5 miles before picking up a gravel road south of the Goose Creek Flooding. As the trail reaches Goose Creek Road, hikers will step out of Kalkaska County and into Crawford County.

Less than 0.5 mile northeast is the next campground, Goose Creek Camp. The forested area and open spaces hikers pass through before reaching the campground are remnants of an old logging camp. The campsite is on the banks of the Manistee River.

From Goose Creek Camp, the trail takes a southeast heading to pass between Lake Margrethe and the town of Grayling before bending back toward the east. The path heads south for 3 miles and crosses Batterson Road, sharing a short 1-mile stretch of state forest road. It then curves south and again goes cross-country for a 3-mile hike to the next series of gravel roads; this section leads to M–72, which hikers must cross.

From the highway crossing, the trail continues south for another 5.5 miles to Four Mile Road. Hikers have the graded shoulders of Four Mile Road as a pathway for the next 9 miles as the trace heads due east. About 4.8 miles after stepping onto Four Mile Road, tired hikers find Four Mile Camp, which appears on the right. This large campsite has all the necessities for a pleasant night's stay.

From the campground, the trail continues east for another 5 miles along Four Mile Road (which hikers by now feel is misnamed) to the intersection with Chase Bridge Road. Crossing this latter road, the trail continues east along a series of narrow, sandy roads. It goes 4.5 miles in this way, until it intersects with M–72 once more. The trail crosses to the north side of the highway and shadows the roadway for the next 4 miles before crossing back to the south side. The terrain here is a bit hilly and the trail is sandy because of the use by horses, but with a little patience it can be easily negotiated. Keep an eye out for rare Kirtland warblers through this area.

About 1 mile south of M–72, the pathway again takes an eastern heading as it trails toward the next campsite, at Luzerne Camp, 6.5 miles from this turn. The trail passes over a series of rolling hills covered by mixed pines and hardwoods. Two miles after making the eastern swing, hikers enter Oscoda County.

From Luzerne Camp, the pathway meanders east, following a series of two-track roads and forest roads to cross M–33 about 5 miles south of the city of Mio. The trail shadows the right shoulder of the highway for about 1 mile before resuming its northeast meander toward Lake Huron.

Nearly 7 miles farther on, hikers will cross Forest Road 4146, staying on the north side of the road for about 2 miles before crossing back to the south to continue the eastward trek. Midway along that 2-mile stretch of the trail, McKinley Camp appears on the left, along the southern banks of the Au Sable River.

The remainder of the hike is along the Au Sable River and its wide, forested valley. After crossing FR 4146, the trail shadows the Au Sable River for 8 miles as it makes its way south toward Alcona Pond. Hikers cross into Alcona County about 2.5 miles before reaching the pond. The trail traces the western and southern shores of the impoundment for nearly 3 miles before swinging southeast for the 3.5 miles to the Iosco County line.

The next campground, South Branch Trail Camp, is just 1.25 miles farther along the trail. From the campground, the trail continues southeast for 4 miles until it crosses Rollaway Road, crossing Michigan Highway 65 in 0.25 mile. The path directs itself more easterly once across the highway, shadowing M–65 for about 5 miles before staying on the high ridges above River Road, a National Scenic Byway segment that runs east all the way into Oscoda. After crossing Forest Road 4421, the roadway to your left is River Road. The trail and the roadway both lead to the same place, so if the trail has become too much, the shoulder of the road will deliver you to the same destination.

About 7.5 miles farther east, the trail crosses River Road, continuing on the northern side along the bank of the Au Sable River. The trail stays on this side of the roadway for the next 6 miles before it crosses back to the southern side of the roadway. The final campsite along the Shore-to-Shore Trail is located 0.1 mile past that crossover, but you must recross River Road to enter Old Orchard Park Camp.

The final 11 miles to Oscoda will seem tame after hiking the previous 200-plus; the trail levels out with few hills left to conquer before reaching the shores of Lake Huron. As you sit on the sand of the lakeshore and think over your cross-state trek, it won't take much to figure out just why the fur traders used water routes.

Key points:

- **7.0** Garey Lake Camp
- **22.0** DuBonnett Camp
- **38.2** Mayfield
- **40.7** Scheck's Trail Camp
- **54.5** Kalkaska Camp
- **65.0** Goose Creek Camp
- **91.8** Four Mile Camp
- **112.0** Luzerne Camp
- **165.5** South Branch Trail Camp
- **185.5** River Road
- **209.0** Old Orchard Park Camp

Waterloo and Pinckney State Recreation Areas

T he Waterloo–Pinckney Trail links two of southern Michigan's most popular recreation spots: the Waterloo and Pinckney recreation areas, which are easily accessible from all major metropolitan areas of southeastern Michigan and thus are available to the largest segment of the state's population. The Waterloo–Pinckney trail system is one hour driving time west of Detroit and is within two hours of all major urban areas in the heavily populated southern half of the state.

Although the location in urban southern Michigan may seem unappealing to some hikers, the trail carefully avoids any exposure to that environment. The Waterloo–Pinckney Recreation Trail mixes habitats and scenic vistas that rival many other areas of the state. The area holds more than a dozen lakes and a greater number of small streams and creeks within its boundaries, along with upland forests, high ridges, and lowland marshes and bogs, all laced together by a trail system that is both challenging and hikable.

Camping is available along the trail system at designated campsites only. Access points and campgrounds allow hikers to plan a tailor-made trip through the system, but this is not a hike that should be taken lightly despite the easy nature of the pathway. The trails are well marked, but use by other nonmotorized users such as equestrians and mountain bikers can cause some problems—nothing like a traffic jam along the trail! Study maps of the system, plan to use the available campsites to break up the hike into easy segments, and come prepared to enjoy the finest trail system in southern Michigan.

22 Waterloo-Pinckney Recreation Hiking Trail

Highlights: Although not as rugged as trails in the western Upper Peninsula or as remote as Isle Royale, this urban trail system mixes upland and watery habitats with scenic vistas that rival any other area in the state. The trail provides access to perhaps the greatest mix of bird habitats in the region, offering birding opportunities that cannot be found anywhere else in the state in such concentrations.

Type of hike: Backpack linear hike.

Total distance: 36 miles.

Difficulty: Moderate.

Best months: June through October.

Maps: USGS Chelsea, Grass Lake, Gregory, and Pinckney; Michigan Department of Natural Resources trail map entitled "Waterloo-Pinckney Trail."

Permits and fees: Daily state park motor vehicle permit, $4.00; annual permit, $20.00. Camping at Waterloo-Pinckney ranges from $9.00 per night for rustic campsites to $17.00 per night for a modern campsite.

Special considerations: Birding opportunities abound in all seasons.

For more information: Waterloo State Recreation Area Headquarters, 16345 McClure Road, Chelsea, MI 48169; Pinckney State Recreation Area Headquarters, 8555 Silverhill, Pinckney, MI 48169.

Parking and trailhead facilities: There is plenty of parking, but only limited services are available at the two trailheads.

Finding the trailhead: The eastern trailhead is at park headquarters for the Pinckney Recreation Area at the Silver Lake Day Use Area. From Michigan Highway 52 near Pinckney, head east on North Territorial Road for 5 miles to Dexter Townhall Road and turn left. The park entrance will be on the left, about 0.5 mile from the turn.

The western trailhead is at the Portage Lake Day Use Area. From Interstate 94, exit north on Race Road. Drive north for about 1 mile to Seymour Road and turn right. The entrance is on the right, about 0.5 mile after the turn.

The hike:

This moderate-rated hike can be covered in three days, but doing so will require double-digit mileage days on the trail. The 36-mile hike starts in the Portage Lake Day Use Area (western trailhead), near the boat ramps. The trail begins as a level, easy walk along a high point overlooking the southern shores of the lake. The view does not last long, since the trail soon heads south to the first of many road crossings. The trail crosses Seymour Road just about 1 mile from the trailhead and nearly parallels the road for the next 2 miles.

In the next section of trail, hikers cross List and then Willis Roads before reaching Portage Pond. A short footbridge provides access over the dam at the neck of the impoundment; from there the trail swings decidedly south again.

Nearly 1 mile past the pond, hikers cross Glenn Road and start the first of the major climbs along the route. The trail winds along a ridge before dropping quickly, but hikers will start climbing immediately to the highest point along the trail,

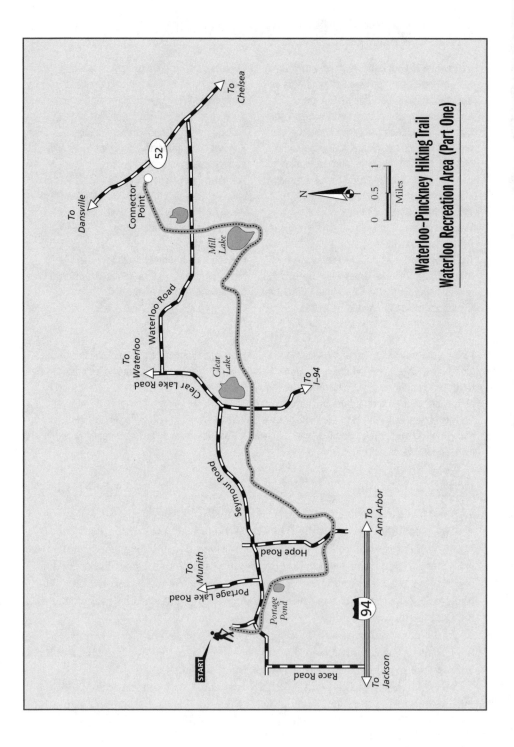

Waterloo–Pinckney Hiking Trail
Waterloo Recreation Area (Part One)

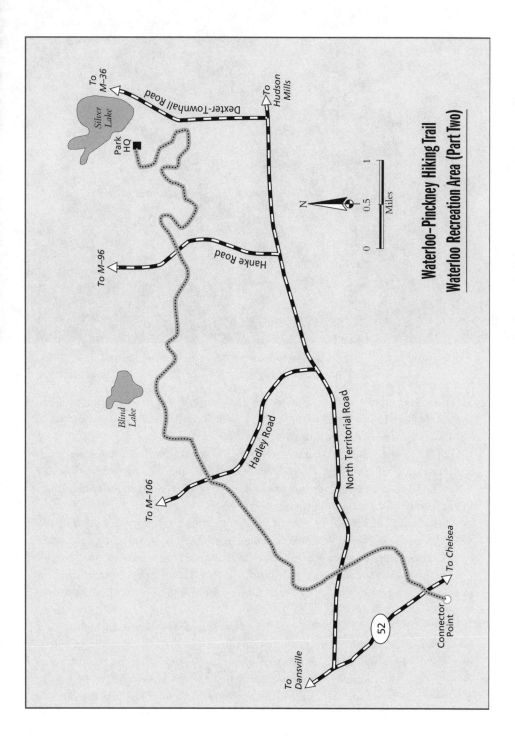

Waterloo–Pinckney Hiking Trail
Waterloo Recreation Area (Part Two)

The cowslip is just one of a myriad spring-blooming species found along the trail.

Sackrider Hill (1,128 feet). From here the trail drops down to level again as hikers shadow Mount Hope Road to its junction with Katz Road, following Katz Road until the trail crosses Glenn Road again.

For the next 5 miles the trail swings north and angles a bit toward the next roadway, Baldwin Road. Bird lovers need to keep cameras and binoculars ready, because a large flooded area in 0.5 mile hosts large numbers of songbirds and waterfowl, providing plenty of viewing opportunities.

Clear Lake Road is the next landmark. Another tough climb awaits 0.5 mile farther. This ascent to Pond Lily Lookout is well worth the effort, providing a nice view of the surrounding countryside. An important landmark appears next, after a quick descent from the lookout: Loveland Road, which is the junction of trails that lead to nearby campgrounds. Sugarloaf Lake Campground is the nearest, 1 mile north of the junction.

The trail continues, crossing McClure Road as it heads eastward. Hikers will cross the road several more times as the trail moves past Crooked Lake and interestingly mixed terrain. The trail now turns southeast, passing along the western shore of Mill Lake, then abruptly swinging north to trace the eastern shore, passing an interpretive center and, later, the Mill Lake Outdoor Center. Just past the outdoor center, hikers will cross Bush Road and start the climb to Waterloo Road. A brief hike brings a totally unexpected sight: PRISON ZONE signs indicate that the Cassidy Lake Correctional Facility is nearby. Obey the signs as you move through this area.

The terrain here is quite hilly, but none of these stretches require strenuous climbs. The trail starts to settle into an easterly direction, crossing Cassidy Lake Road before arriving near the entrance to the Green Lake Campground. From the campground the trail crosses Michigan Highway 52, leaves the Waterloo Recreation Area, and enters Park Lyndon, a Washtenaw County park, for a brief period. This stretch of the trail can be a bit confusing, so keep a sharp eye out for Department of Natural Resources' trail triangles to stay on the main pathway.

Hikers will soon cross North Territorial Road, continue north for 0.5 mile, then swing northeasterly once again. Hikers cross the boundary of the Pinckney Recreation Area at a footbridge over a small creek several hundred yards after the noticeable change in direction. The trail continues to the northeast, crossing Emburn and then Joslip Lake Roads, detouring around a large hill and then a marshy area before crossing Hadley Road. From this point, day-use areas and private cottage communities around several of the larger lakes remind hikers of the region's urban nature. The trail from here is fairly hilly in several spots, but even the most tired of hikers can make quick work of the final few miles to the eastern trailhead at the Silver Lake Day Use Area.

Key points:

10.5 Sugarloaf Lake Campground
14.0 Green Lake Campground
15.0 M-52
21.0 Hadley Road (marshy area)

Weekend
Hikes

Cedar River Country

The Cedar River Pathway is made up of four loops ranging from 2 to 7 miles. These are easy hikes for explorers of all ages. The pathway is made up of four loops—2 miles, 3.5 miles, 5 miles, and 7 miles long—which offer hikers the opportunity to explore. The trails are wide, well marked, and easy to follow through a mix of upland and lowland habitats that provide plenty of diversions. Trails follow many of the ridgelines that crisscross the area, as well as "glacier tracks," or eskers, left behind by retreating sheets of ice.

The western edges of the trail system trace a portion of the Cedar River, the area's greatest attraction. From the fifteen-site rustic campground on the banks of the Cedar River to fishing opportunities, wildlife, and wildflowers, the area is a step into the nature of the region.

The easy-to-follow trails usually provide a smooth adventure into typical Upper Peninsula river habitat, although the total distance of the trail loops can make this a moderate hike for inexperienced hikers. Pace yourself. There are several opportunities to cut the 7-mile hike short if bad weather or other misfortunes arise. The rustic campground located at the southern end of the trails provides a great spot to end the day.

23 Cedar River Pathway

Highlights: A 15-site rustic campground, terrific trout fishing, wildlife, and wildflowers are all part of the lure of this remote western Upper Peninsula trail. With the Cedar River as a backdrop and a blend of upland and riverine environments, this is a special place for the hiker seeking a little solitude along what some rate as the finest loop trail system in Michigan.

Type of hike: Loop hike.

Total distance: 7 miles.

Difficulty: Easy.

Best months: August through October.

Map: The Michigan Department of Natural Resources Field Office in Gladstone distributes a more than adequate trail map.

Permits and fees: None.

Special considerations: Big and small game hunters use the area extensively starting in late September.

For more information: Forester, Escanaba River State Forest, 6833 U.S. Highway 41, Gladstone, MI 49837; (906) 786-2351; Forest Fire Officer, Department of Natural Resources, Stephenson, MI 49987; (906) 753-6317.

Parking and trailhead facilities: Parking is very limited in the campground and is reserved for campers. The small parking lot east of the campground can accommodate a limited number of vehicles.

Finding the trailhead: The trailhead can be reached from three major highways in the western Upper Peninsula: U.S. Highway 2 from the north; Michigan Highway 35 from the south; and U.S. 41 from the west. All three will connect with River Road (County Road 551) leading to the turnoff to the trail and a nearby campground. From the turn off River Road, hikers have two options: One trailhead is located adjacent to a parking lot east of the Cedar River Campground; and the other is at the northern edge of the campground.

The hike:

From the campground, which is the start point for most hikers using the trail system, the **2-mile loop** moves quickly to the northeast, away from the river. About 0.4 mile from the trailhead, hikers reach a junction with the 3.5-mile loop. This longer loop swings back toward the Cedar River, while the shorter loop swings east for nearly 0.3 mile to its return leg and junction for the second loop in the trail system. A bench located at the junction of these two trails marks the halfway point. There are benches along the entire 7 miles of the trail, placed primarily for cross-country skiers but enjoyed every bit as much by hikers. Just past the bench the smallest loop swings south for the 0.5 mile trek to the access road leading into the campground. Once at the road, hikers will swing back west and use the roadway for the return trip to the campground and the trailhead. Although this is not a major thoroughfare, hikers are warned to keep their eyes open for traffic.

Loop 2, the **3.5-mile loop,** offers a pleasant walk along the banks of the Cedar River. It picks up at the junction with the small loop mentioned above and presses northwest, making one small detour south before heading for the banks of the river.

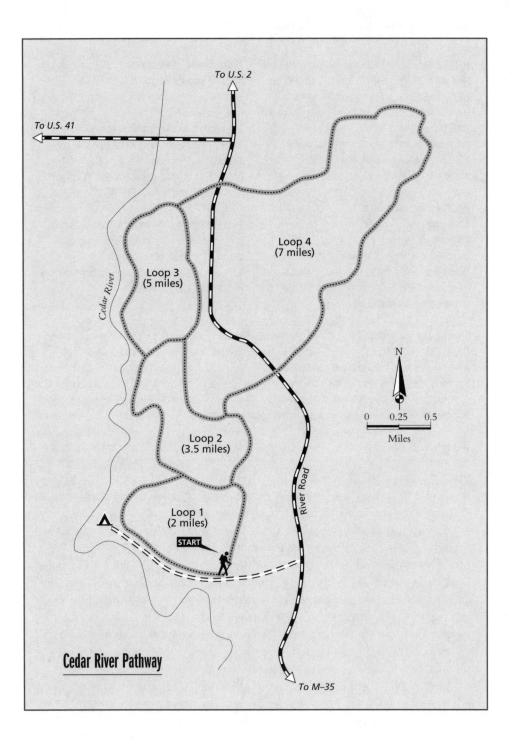

To U.S. 2

To U.S. 41

Cedar River

Loop 4
(7 miles)

Loop 3
(5 miles)

Loop 2
(3.5 miles)

River Road

Loop 1
(2 miles)

START

N

0   0.25   0.5
Miles

Cedar River Pathway

To M–35

Fall hikers are advised to wear bright colors as they walk the trails, since the area is used heavily by woodcock and grouse hunters.

Another rest-stop bench is located on the riverbank, about 0.4 mile from the start of this second loop. From the bench, the trail continues north for 0.2 mile to the outbound junction with Loop 3, before bending east for another 0.2 mile to the inbound junction with that loop. Hikers on the 3.5-mile loop head south, then east, for 0.5 mile to a junction with the largest of the four loops, the 7-mile leg of the Cedar River Pathway. It is only about 0.3 mile from this junction to another junction with the first small loop.

Tracing Loop 3, the **5-mile loop** in this system, offers hikers nearly 0.75 mile of trail along the river. At the top of the loop, hikers swing briefly east away from the river to the outbound junction with the larger 7-mile loop in the system. From this junction, hikers head nearly due south for 0.7 mile to the junction with the 3.5-mile loop and the return trip to trailhead. You also have another option: if the river holds a special fascination for you, a right turn and 0.2-mile hike will take you back to the start point for the loop. Taking this route, you can trace the western edges of the pathway and stay along the riverbank for the return trip to the trailhead.

Loop 4, the **7-mile pathway**, starts at the top of the 5-mile loop and heads generally east for 0.25 mile where the trail crosses River Road for the first time. After crossing the road the trail heads northeast for 0.75 mile to another trailside bench before swinging back to the southwest. About 0.75 mile later the trail crosses River

Road again, continuing for 0.25 mile to the junction with the return leg of the 3.5-mile loop in the system.

Hikers have several options at this point, depending on time and the condition of their tired feet. You can turn right at the junction and backtrack on the 3.5-mile loop to the river, then trace the river back to the campground. Or you can turn left and hike to the junction with the 2-mile loop, then make a right turn to backtrack on that trail to the campground. Another option is to simply keep bearing left through all the junctions and complete the long loop called the Cedar River Pathway.

There is one other lengthy detour that you could take: turn right at the outer end of the 7-mile loop, backtrack the 3.5-mile and 5-mile loops, and return to the campground by retracing your outbound trek along the river. Only time and energy limit the possibilities.

Key points:

Three trails—2-mile, 3.5-mile, and 5-mile loops—shadow the Cedar River. The larger 7-mile loop is east of the river and will actually cross River Road twice during its meanderings.

Seney National Wildlife Refuge

The primary purpose of the vast Seney National Wildlife Refuge is the management of wildlife and its habitat. But included in the plan to preserve the area is an idea of balanced use, and that includes a variety of wildlife-oriented recreational opportunities. The refuge offers several clearly defined trails and roadways that offer the hiker 70 miles of possible loops and linear hikes to all corners of the area.

The Seney National Wildlife Refuge includes more than two dozen pools, several of which are artificially controlled to create nesting or feeding areas for a variety of waterfowl and birds common to the region. It is one of the few "wilderness" areas that permit vehicles, although these are limited to a 7-mile, self-guided marshland road that is also open to hikers and bikers.

The only scenic views here are those of the open pools and marsh grass flats; wildlife viewing is the main attraction. Visitors may see many species of birds, including waterfowl and raptors. Migrating ducks and geese use the refuge as a rest stop, but large numbers of Canada geese use the area as a nursery. Loons, sandhill cranes, trumpeter swans, eagles, and osprey also use the bounty of the refuge to feed their young. White-tailed deer, beaver, and otter are abundant in the area, but there are also black bear, coyote, bobcat, and three species of grouse in the confines of the refuge. The refuge hosts annual butterfly and wildflower outings.

Trails in the refuge are firm-surfaced gravel routes that carve through the interior of the area and between pools. The 70 miles of road and trail give hikers the chance to customize a trek depending on how much time they have. No camping is permitted in the refuge, so plan hikes that allow for time to return to your vehicle for the trip back to the campground. There is no fresh water or other conveniences along the refuge trails.

The refuge is managed by the U.S. Fish & Wildlife Service, with its visitor center remaining open for much of the snow-free period, May through September.

24 Seney National Wildlife Refuge Trails

Highlights: The Seney National Wildlife Refuge is in a quiet corner of the eastern Upper Peninsula. The area permits visitors to peek into the marsh and wetland habitats typical of the region.

Type of hike: Loop hike.

Total distance: 70 miles.

Difficulty: Easy to moderate.

Best months: The refuge is open to hikers May through September.

Maps: Visitor center staff can provide an excellent map of the trails/roadways in the refuge. Markers along the routes make the hikes easy to follow.

Permits and fees: None.

Special considerations: Hikers entering the refuge in May and June will have to deal with mosquitoes and blackflies. Only nine of the pools and ponds in the refuge are open to fishing, so check at the visitor center for the latest regulations.

For more information: Seney National Wildlife Refuge Manager, HCR #2, Box 1, Seney, MI 49883, (906) 586-9851.

Parking and trailhead facilities: The parking lot at the visitor center is paved and can easily handle two dozen cars or more. A few vending machines are located at the center, but other amenities will have to be brought along.

Finding the trailhead: There are several entrances to the refuge, but the common start point for hikers is the refuge visitor center a short drive west of Michigan Highway 77. The paved entrance road winds 0.5 mile west to the trailhead.

The hikes:

The nearly 70 miles of well-developed forest roads in Seney National Wildlife Refuge provide limited access for vehicular traffic and more access for bicyclists and hikers. The one trail set aside specifically for hikers is the 1.4-mile **Pine Ridge Nature Trail,** a walk along a portion of the dike system supporting several of the pools in the refuge. The trail is flat, wide, and well marked. It heads east from the visitor center and eventually traces the shores of a large pool that is home to Canada geese, loons, and a few trumpeter swans before returning to the start point.

Marshland Wildlife Drive is a 7-mile trip deeper into the heart of the refuge, offering visitors a look at a major part of the management system and diverse habitat within a wetland area. One-way vehicle traffic on the pathway ensures that hikers won't be surprised by a car, but they will have to share the route. The first mile of path traces the southern shore of F Pool, climbing around the southern shoreline in several minor bumps before dropping back down to trace the eastern and southern shore of E Pool. To the uninitiated, it may seem that there are loons everywhere, but the most prominent flying creatures in the refuge are the small, biting variety! Plan to stop at the Swan Observation Deck and scan the pool for signs of waterfowl.

The most noticeable feature of the region is the wonderful earthy smell of the marsh that continuously surrounds you. The next portion of the Marshland Drive

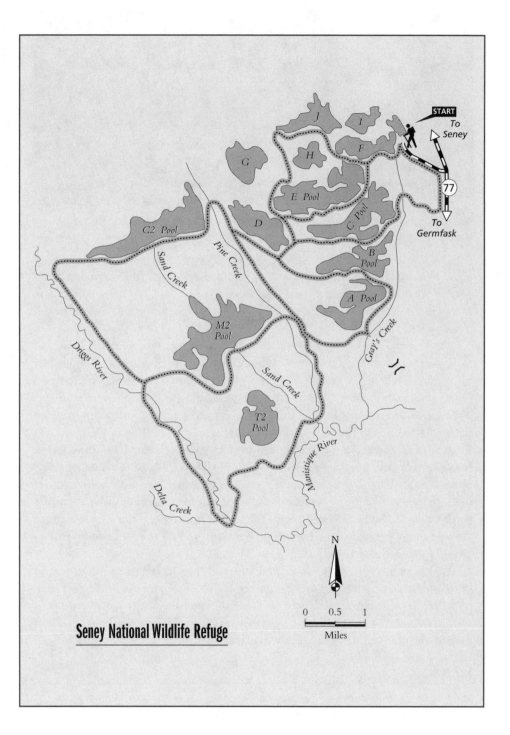

START
To
Seney

To
Germfask

77

J
I
F
G
H
E Pool
C Pool
D
B
Pool
A Pool
C2 Pool
Pine Creek
Sand Creek
M2
Pool
Sand Creek
Driggs River
Gray's Creek
T2
Pool
Manistique River
Delta Creek

N

0   0.5   1
Miles

Seney National Wildlife Refuge

Seney National Wildlife Refuge is a blend of upland, marsh, and wetland habitats typical of the central Upper Peninsula and home to a variety of wildlife, including red fox.

pathway stretches for 2 miles westward to its junction with the Fishing Loop. From here the trail heads south along the eastern shore of D Pool, offering hikers a look from the Loon Observation Deck before swinging nearly due east for the final 4 miles to M–77.

Much of the remainder of the trip is spent passing between C and B Pools, but make sure you stop at the Eagle Nest Observatory for a peek at an active eagle's nest on the far side of the pool. There are also plenty of ducks and geese on these two pools, along with wading shorebirds that nest along the grassy shores. Keep your eyes open for small mammals feeding in the shallows and for the painted and snapping turtles that inhabit the pools.

Two other routes through the refuge are **Driggs River Road** and **Pine Creek Road,** both open to nonmotorized traffic only. Driggs River Road is accessible from Michigan Highway 28, 7.5 miles west of Seney, but park managers recommend that you use the Marshland Wildlife Drive route to access this pathway at a junction point between D and C Pools; this will also serve as access to Pine Creek Road, a 10-mile linear pathway with two connector trails leading to the 18-mile trace of Driggs River Road.

A good number of smaller loops and spur trails provide access to the remainder of the two dozen pools deep in the confines of the refuge. Although refuge officials recommend a side trip along a ridge or along the top of a dike to get a better view of wildlife and the many birds that call Seney home, remember that this is a wet and tangled environment that can quickly disorient a hiker.

Key points:

The ponds in the refuge attract the most attention, since they are nesting areas home to a wide variety of migratory waterfowl and shorebirds.

Fox River Pathway

E rnest Hemingway based his fabled *Big Two Hearted River* saga on his exploits along this classic eastern Upper Peninsula trout stream. The trout fishing is still as good as it was when Hemingway visited the area, and the Fox River Pathway shadows the Fox and then the Little Fox Rivers for nearly the entire length of its route from Seney to Kingston Lake Campground.

This moderate-to-difficult hike is a point-to-point trek that ends just 4 miles short of the Pictured Rocks National Lakeshore. Any hiker attempting the trek should be in good physical shape because of the nature of the terrain. You will need to allow extra time to rest feet and muscles if you intend to complete the hike in three or four days' time. Be sure to wear good boots to deal with the changing footing along the length of the route.

The trail parallels waterways for much of its length. It passes through stands of jack pine and the remnants of a boom-and-bust logging era that left its mark on the region, including the foundations of old logging camps, railroad grades long abandoned, and dams created to provide water for floating logs down to Seney. Forest fires finished the job of reseeding much of the area along the trail; the red pine plantations seen along the way were planted in the mid-1950s as part of an effort to plant more than twenty million pines in the Shingleton Forest Area. Although logging is the region's heritage, trout fishing in the Fox River attracts more people today. Wildlife abounds in the Singleton Forest and includes deer and black bear, as well as all sorts of small game and birdlife. In the fall, ducks and geese stop to use the river and the floodings along the system.

The trail opens up recreational opportunities in a large area. Hikers have several more trip options at its terminus, one of which is joining the North Country Trail. Keep in mind that this is a linear trail; hikers must make arrangements for transportation back to the trailhead or plan on retracing steps back to the start.

The trail passes through the remnants of a bygone logging era—tangles of downed timber and stumps laced together by trickles and creeks that can spell trouble for a careless hiker.

25 Fox River Pathway

Highlights: This trail will transport you back to a time when logging was king and nature, not man, ruled the region.

Type of hike: Backpack linear hike.

Total distance: 27.5 miles.

Difficulty: Moderate to difficult.

Best months: Late summer to fall.

Map: The Department of Natural Resources Shingleton Field Office provides an excellent map and trail brochure on the trail system, complete with mile markers and other useful information.

Permits and fees: None.

Special considerations: Although trout season opens in spring and is why many hikers are drawn to the waterway, the squadrons of mosquitoes and blackflies hatched in early spring make this one hike to avoid unless you are determined to be an insect blood donor. The terrain and environments make this a tough hike, so be prepared to slow your pace a bit.

For more information: Area Forester, Shingleton Forest Area, Michigan Highway 28 (M-28), Shingleton, MI 49884; District Forest Manager, Lake Superior State Forest, P.O. Box 445, Newberry, MI 49868; Department of Natural Resources, P.O. Box 67, Shingleton, MI 49884; (906) 452-6227.

Parking and trailhead facilities: Parking at the trailhead is somewhat limited but adequate, since the trail does not attract crowds. Water is available at the campground, but other needs must be administered to prior to setting out on the trek.

Finding the trailhead: The trailhead is at the Seney Township Campground north of the Fox River Bridge, just north of Seney on M-28. Once across the bridge, turn right onto Fox River Road. The campground is about 0.25 mile ahead on the right.

The hike:

The trail generally parallels the Fox River and the Little Fox River for the first 17 miles before heading cross-country the remaining 10 miles to Kingston Lake Campground. Between resting and fishing, hikers will find that the days slip by rather quickly.

From the Seney Township Campground, the trail heads west for 0.8 mile to the first of many stands of jack pine you will encounter along the trail. This stand extends for nearly 5 miles as you move along, then away from, the Fox River to navigate around blocks of private property. At Two Mile Ditch hikers swing back north and head once again for the river, slightly more than 3 miles away. The ditches here were dug just after the turn of the twentieth century as part of a plan to develop farms in the area; the plan failed, and the state assumed ownership of the land. At the end of this leg you will cross Fox River Road and enter the Fox River Plains, shadowing the rivers for the next 12 miles.

About 1 mile past the road crossing, you will find the first recommended stop along the trail, the Fox River Campground. Registration cards can be found on the

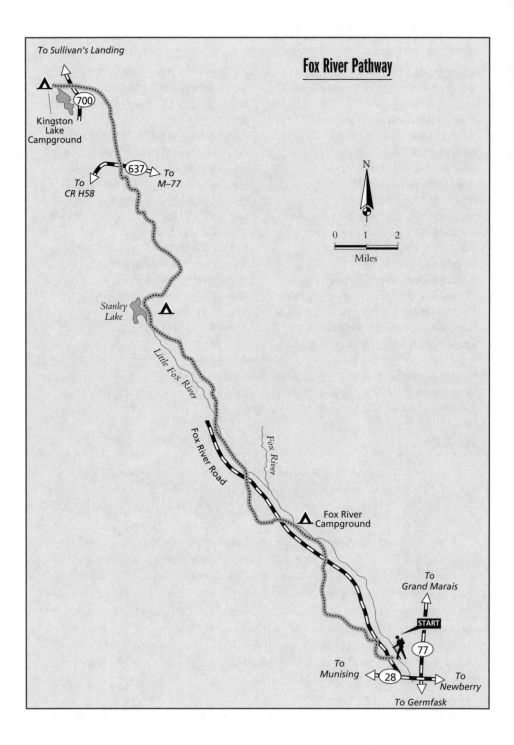

Fox River Pathway

information board at the entrance to campsites. You must register your campsite—and remember to take out everything you carried in.

The next 2 miles of trail cross through a nearly twenty-year-old cutting of mature jack pine. Hikers will pass the remnants of a logging camp built in the late 1880s, walking back into the rich history of the region. Since the lumber heyday, a total of twenty million trees have been planted in the Singleton Forest Area, a large portion of which grow along the flanks of the Fox River.

The trail crosses Fox River Road again but this time follows the course of the Little Fox River northwest. Hikers must cross the river using an old truck trail. About 0.5 mile from the crossing, you will find one of eight water-control dams built along the Fox River system to regulate and store water for the loggers so that they could float timber downstream to Seney. Nearly 2 miles farther you will encounter a hill that was cut down so that loggers could more easily move logs along an old sleigh road.

From here it's 4 miles to Stanley Lake Dam and the Stanley Lake Campground. Fishing enthusiasts looking for a break from stream fishing can try their luck with the abundant northern pike in these slack waters. A 0.6-mile spur trail takes you along the shore of Stanley Lake, then right back to the pathway.

From here until the trail reaches Clyde Lake, 5 miles farther on, the terrain is a bit soggy as you pass through a series of berry bogs. The trail shadows the West Branch of the Fox River for a short time before heading back north. After passing Clyde, Fishhook, and Ewatt Lakes, the trail crosses County Road 637. From the crossing it is 4.2 miles through the Kingston Plains and what locals refer to as a "stump museum," a collection of still-standing burned snags and stumps left behind by loggers in the late 1880s.

The trail swings west near the end to avoid private property and crosses County Road 700 just prior to entering the campground. If you continue north on CR 700 for 4 miles, you will reach the Pictured Rocks National Lakeshore's Twelve-Mile Beach Campground. Once there you can connect with the Pictured Rocks trail system. If you turn right at the campground, Grand Marais is only 11 miles away. Turn left to reach Munising in 24 miles.

Key points:

6.0	Two Mile Ditch
9.5	Fox River
11.5	Fox River Campground
15.25	Stanley Lake Campground
20.5	Clyde Lake
24.5	Kingston Plains "Stump Museum"
27.0	County Road 700

Sleeping Bear Dunes National Lakeshore

T he Sleeping Bear Dunes National Lakeshore is an area of stunning dunes, forests, and wetlands about 8 miles northeast of Glen Arbor in central Leelanau County, between Lake Michigan and the north shore of Little Traverse Lake. The Sleeping Bear Dunes region is a multiuse area and, except for riders of mechanized devices, open to everyone with a desire to explore the dunes along the Lake Michigan shoreline. The entire area was submerged under Ancestral Lake Michigan about 11,000 years ago and has gradually emerged. The Chippewa Indians gave birth to the legends that created the Sleeping Bear name.

Low ridges along the shoreline are punctuated by wetlands. Loops and connector trails within the area offer an all-day outing or a quick look at the landscape of the countryside and offshore islands, including North and South Manitou Islands. Few trails in the park are long enough to fill an entire day, but each trail listed in this section offers a different look at the mix of environments.

Most trails are easily handled by even the casual hiker, but the sandy trails throughout the area can be tough on feet if you have ill-fitting footwear. On trails along the Sleeping Bear Dunes, heavy hiking boots should be left behind in favor of the new lightweight boots or high-top sneakers.

26 Good Harbor Bay Loop

Highlights: A short loop trail through diverse habitats—dunes, forests, wetlands, and shore-line.

Type of hike: Loop hike.

Total distance: 2.8 miles.

Difficulty: Easy to moderate.

Best months: August through October.

Map: National Park Service area map.

Permits and fees: Sleeping Bear Dunes Park Pass: $7.00 for 7 days; $15.00 for 12 months (from date of purchase, not a calen-

dar year). Camping is available at D. H. Day Campground for $10 per night.

Special considerations: Birding and scenic dunes.

For more information: Sleeping Bear Dunes Lakeshore, 9922 Front Street, Empire, MI 49630-9797; headquarters and visitor information; (231) 326-5134.

Parking and trailhead facilities: There is adequate parking at the trailhead.

Finding the trailhead: From Glen Arbor, drive north for about 8 miles on Michigan Highway 22 to County Road 669. Turn left and drive about 1.5 miles to Lake Michigan Road. Turn right and continue for about 1 mile to the trailhead on the right.

The hike:

The 2.8-mile Good Harbor Bay Loop traces more of a square than a circle. It moves through sandy dunes and wooded fringe areas, then into a wetland habitat that borders the southern leg of the trail, then woodlands, and, finally, the sand shores of Lake Michigan again.

From the trailhead, the trail heads east through the dunes that make the region so attractive to visitors. This is the toughest part of the trail, since footing can be unstable on nothing more than shifting sand. The trail goes east for about 0.4 mile, then turns south, moving out of the dunes and into a forested area for nearly 0.5 mile before giving way to the wettest area of the loop.

Hikers will cross a small footbridge over a ribbon of water as they head for the next corner of the trail. The trail switches back to the west about 1 mile into the wetlands. This stretch of the trail is especially interesting during the spring because of the diverse wildflowers found along the trail. At the end of this leg, a short board-walk carries hikers across the wettest section.

The western leg of the trail swings due north for about 0.6 mile through a forested area that offers shade in summer and a look at the backbone of the entire dunes area.

At the end of this leg, the trail swings due east for the final few hundred yards to the trailhead. The picnic area east of the trailhead is a terrific spot to rest those weary feet and relax before moving on to the next trail in the Sleeping Bear Dunes.

Key points:

The four sides of this "square" loop trail are each about 0.75 mile long, with the trailhead located midway along the northern leg.

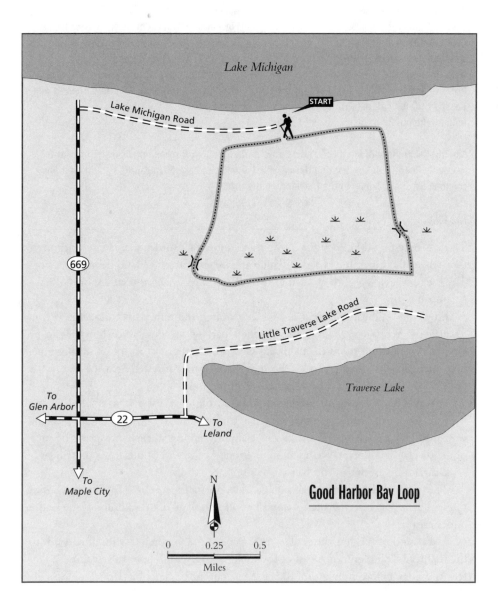

Good Harbor Bay Loop

Although its namesake suggests a dry region, Sleeping Bear Dunes is home to large areas of wetlands and other ecosystems.

27 Pyramid Point Loop

Highlights: Spectacular vistas throughout what is probably the most remote corner of Sleeping Bear Dunes National Lakeshore.
Type of hike: Loop hike.
Total distance: 2.8 miles.
Difficulty: Moderate.
Best months: August through October.
Maps: USGS Glen Arbor; Pyramid Point Trail map, free of charge at the visitor center.
Permits and fees: Sleeping Bear Dunes Park Pass: $7.00 for 7 days; $15.00 for 12 months (from date of purchase, not a calendar year). Camping is available at D. H. Day

Campground for $10 per night.
Special considerations: Lookout Point, from which hikers can see the shipwreck of the *Morazan,* South Manitou Island and its lighthouse, North Manitou Island, the Manitou Shoals, South Fox Island, and Pyramid Point.
For more information: Sleeping Bear Dunes Lakeshore, 9922 Front Street, Empire, MI 49630-9797; headquarters and visitor information, (231) 326-5134.
Parking and trailhead facilities: There is adequate parking at the trailhead.

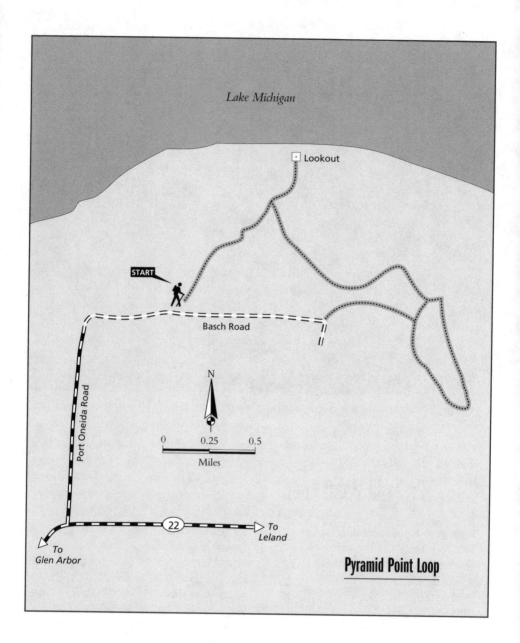

Lake Michigan

Lookout

START

Basch Road

Port Oneida Road

N

0   0.25   0.5
Miles

22

To
Leland

To
Glen Arbor

Pyramid Point Loop

Finding the trailhead: From Glen Arbor, drive north for 5 miles on Michigan Highway 22. As the highway turns decidedly east, you will make a left turn onto Port Oneida Road. Drive north for 2 miles to Basch Road and turn right. The dirt road you turn onto will continue on for about 300 yards to the trailhead.

The hike:

The Pyramid Point Loop blends all the various environments that make up the Sleeping Bear Dunes National Lakeshore with spectacular vistas as far as the eye can see.

From the trailhead the hike meanders toward the sandy shoreline of Lake Michigan along a deserted two-track road and over glacial moraines that have given root to a beech-and-maple forest. The trees act as barriers against winds off the lake. The hike for the first few hundred yards is through a fairly level meadow, but the trail begins to climb as you near the trees.

For the next 0.25 mile the climb becomes more noticeable as you enter a mixed grove of hardwoods that in summer provides a bit of shade and in fall is ablaze with color. About midway through this forest belt is a trail junction; a short, 0.2-mile spur path leads to Lookout Point, a spectacular vantage point used as a hang glider launch site. The hike is decidedly uphill and the footing not all that stable, but the trek is worth it.

After you take in the phenomenal view, retrace your steps to the junction and head east for 0.6 mile to the next posted junction in the trail. From here hikers have the option of shortening the loop by nearly a mile or continuing on the complete loop through this quiet corner of the dunes area. The main trail drops more than 100 feet in elevation, eventually breaking out of the trees and into another large meadow. The trail swings southeast from the junction, through the meadow, then back northwest toward the trailhead. Only about 0.25 mile of the loop passes through open meadow. Hikers reenter the trees for the 0.6-mile leg to Basch Road. The final 0.4 mile back to the trailhead is a walk along Basch Road; hikers should keep an eye out for traffic.

Key points:

0.6 Lookout Point spur trail junction

1.2 Junction for extended loop or return point to Basch Road. The loop and the shortcut eventually return to Basch Road for the trek back to the trailhead.

28 Bay View Hiking Trails

Highlights: Meanders through mature beech and maple forests and places the magnificent sand dunes at the feet of hikers once they reach Lookout Point.

Type of hike: Loop hike.

Total distance: 9 miles.

Difficulty: Moderate.

Best months: August through October.

Map: National Park Service area map.

Permits and fees: Sleeping Bear Dunes Park Pass: $7.00 for 7 days; $15.00 for 12 months (from date of purchase, not a calendar year). Camping is available at D. H. Day Campground for $10 per night.

Special considerations: Lookout Point, from which hikers can see the shipwreck of the *Morazan*, South Manitou Island and its lighthouse, North Manitou Island, the Manitou Shoals, South Fox Island, and Pyramid Point.

For more information: Sleeping Bear Dunes Lakeshore, 9922 Front Street, Empire, MI 49630-9797; headquarters, (231) 326-5134; visitor information, (231) 326-5134.

Parking and trailhead facilities: Parking is adequate at either trailhead.

Finding the trailhead: Bay View trails are accessible from two trailheads: For the Thorson trailhead, drive 4 miles north of Glen Arbor on Michigan Highway 22 and turn left onto Thorson Road. The trailhead is 0.5 mile ahead on the left. For the Homestead trailhead, drive 2 miles north of Glen Arbor on M-22 to Homestead Resort. The trailhead is just north of the resort on the right side of the road.

The hikes:

The Bay View Hiking Trail, one of the longer trails in the Sleeping Bear Dunes National Lakeshore, comprises four separate loops. The northernmost loop provides an outstanding view of the Lake Michigan shoreline and several offshore islands. The trail offers a mix of environments, including mature forests and the sandy dunes that give the area its name and appeal. Trailheads at opposite ends of the trail offer convenient access to visitors arriving from north or south. All loops are accessible from either trailhead.

The most popular loop in the system is the **Lookout Point Loop,** a 2.4-mile trail to the north of the Thorson trailhead. The trail leads through a series of low sandy hills and open grassy areas that set the mood for the lakeshore and its namesake, but none of the obstacles are considered more than moderate in difficulty. From the trailhead, the trail heads north for 0.4 mile to the junction with a 0.1-mile spur trail to the lookout. Once atop the lookout, you will have—on a clear day—a view of South Manitou Island and its lighthouse, North Manitou Island, the Manitou Shoals Beacon, South Fox Island, and Pyramid Point. Returning to the loop, hikers will head north for about 0.1 mile before turning decidedly east and heading that way for nearly 1 mile. Then the trail shadows M-22, crosses Thorson Road, and

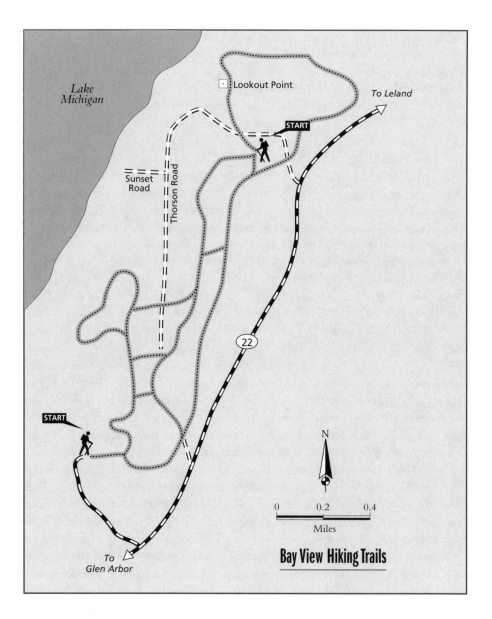

Bay View Hiking Trails

heads back to the trailhead. According to park officials, this loop is not only the most popular in the Bay View system but also the least confusing.

Meadow Trail, High Trail, and **Low Trail** offer configurations that allow hikers to customize treks to match timetables. These loops, with the exception of the Meadow Trail, can be confusing; refer to your map often to remain on the trail you intend to follow. Finding yourself 3 or 4 miles from where you thought you were, with no water and sore feet, is not a pleasant climax to a great day on the trails.

The southern half of the three loops south of the Thorson trailhead offer some shade in mixed hardwood forest, but trails are still sandy and footing isn't all that solid. The three southern loops range in length from 2 to 2.5 miles and offer more options than one could hike in a weekend. Combining portions of the various loops will create a hike that easily fits into a day's outing and doesn't tax your enthusiasm to the point of apathy. Two recommended hikes: combine portions of the Meadow Loop and High Trail or, for a longer hike, combine the High and Low Trails.

The first loop is a 4-mile hike through the southern end of the trail system; the extended hike is a 4.5-mile hike through the length of the system and can easily be combined with a visit to Lookout Point at the north end of the loop. From the Homestead trailhead, both trails share the same 0.2-mile start, taking hikers on an easterly heading to reach the main pathways.

For the **Meadow–High Trails Loop:** Turn left at the 0.2-mile junction and make a snakelike meander for 0.5 mile to the first of three connector trails that only seem to serve to confuse many hikers. Advice from park officials: stay to the left. The first two connector trails, 0.1 and 0.2 mile long respectively, provide shortcuts to the return leg of this 4-mile loop. At a junction with a 0.1-mile spur trail, the main pathway bears to the left, looping 1 mile through a mix of forest and open sandy fields. That loop returns to the main pathway at the junction with the spur-trail shortcut and bends east for the 0.3-mile hike to the junction with the High Trail. The Meadow–High Trails loop then turns south for 0.5 mile, then follows Thorson Road for the next 0.6 mile. Watch the right side of the roadway for the signs pointing the way back to the Homestead trailhead. From the signs, the hike swings back west for 0.4 mile to the spur trail back to the trailhead.

The **High–Low Trails Loop:** This loop retraces the final 1.7 miles of the Meadow–High Trails Loop, actually backtracking to the point where Meadow Trail joins the High Trail. Just beyond this point the trees give way to meadows and stretches of sand; the trail meanders over low hills. The junction with the first connector trail appears on the right, just 0.2 mile from the junction with Meadow Trail; this 0.2-mile spur leads to the return leg along the Low Trail. From this point it is another 0.6 mile to the Thorson trailhead, which is a good choice for hikers looking to enjoy the full scenic beauty of the Sleeping Bear Dunes National Lakeshore. From here, you can either turn right and link up with the Low Trail and thus begin the hike back to the Homestead trailhead or take the time to hike the 2.4-mile loop that will carry you to Lookout Point. I recommend the diversion. The view is magnificent.

From the Thorson trailhead, the return leg starts with a short 0.1-mile hike to the junction with the return leg of the Lookout Point Loop. The trail then heads south for 0.4 mile to the eastern end of the connector trail mentioned earlier and continues for 0.9 mile to the junction with Thorson Road. The final 0.6 mile of the

High-Low Trails Loop retraces a portion of the start of the hike, crossing Thorson Road, then returns along the spur trail to the trailhead.

Key points:

The longest of the loops in this system, Lookout Point Loop, is the most popular and easiest to follow. The others—Meadow Trail, High Trail, and Low Trail—although well marked, can be somewhat confusing at times. Watch trail markers and refer to your map.

29 Alligator Hill Trails

Highlights: This offshore trail offers a look at the backside of what retreating glaciers left behind—a mix of field and forest habitats that attract large numbers of birds and other wildlife. In spring the area is carpeted with wildflowers.

Type of hike: Loop hike.

Total distance: 8.3 miles.

Difficulty: Easy to strenuous.

Best months: August through October.

Map: National Park Service area map.

Permits and fees: Sleeping Bear Dunes Park Pass: $7.00 for 7 days; $15.00 for 12 months (from date of purchase, not a calendar year). Camping is available at D. H. Day

Campground for $10 per night.

Special considerations: A unique opportunity to check out the "rest of the story" behind the creation of the dunes area along the Lake Michigan lakeshore. Glacial terrain and eskers, a mix of upland and wetland habitats, wildlife, and seasonal carpets of wildflowers can all be found along this trail.

For more information: Sleeping Bear Dunes Lakeshore, 9922 Front Street, Empire, MI 49630-9797; headquarters, (231) 326-5134; visitor information, (231) 326-5134.

Parking and trailhead facilities: There is adequate parking at the trailhead.

Finding the trailhead: From Empire drive north on Michigan Highway 109 for 9 miles to Stocking Road and turn right. The trailhead is on the left, about 1 mile past the junction. Stocking Road is just east of the entrance to D. H. Day Campground.

The hike:

The Alligator Hill system is one of the few trail systems in Sleeping Bear Dunes National Lakeshore that does not provide a panoramic view of the lakeshore. But these inland trails are just as important in understanding the complete picture of the Sleeping Bear region, offering a look into the nature of the region that was also carved by retreating glaciers and years of wear from lakeshore breezes and Michi-

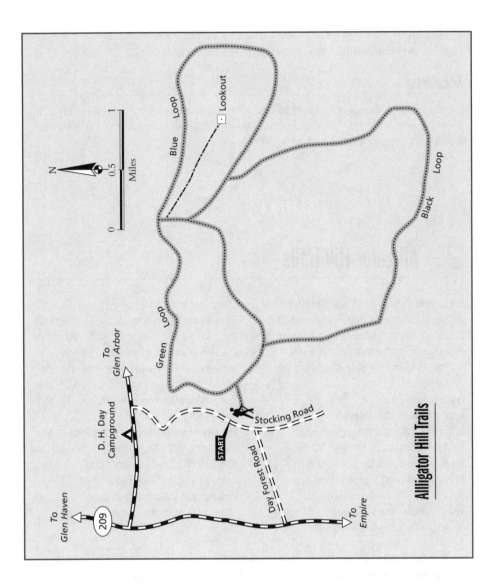

gan winters. The trails weave through a mixture a field and forest habitats that attract large numbers of birds and other wildlife. In springtime the trails are bordered by a rich mixture of wildflowers.

This three-loop trail system has been developed as a hiking-skiing system. Each of its easy-to-follow teardrop-shaped trail loops is 2.5 miles long, and the Blue Loop has an added 0.8-mile spur trail to a patch of high ground that affords a limited view of the surrounding area. The Green and Blue Loops should be hiked counterclockwise; the Black Loop, clockwise.

The mix of ecosystems in the region provides a multitude of spring wildflowers, spreading carpets of color in some areas of the Sleeping Bear Dunes.

From the trailhead off Stocking Road, hikers must start all loops on a portion of the Green Loop. This easy loop heads north for approximately 0.25 mile before turning east for the mile-long hike to the junction with the Blue Loop. Both loops turn south at this point, sharing the next 0.2 mile of trail. About 100 yards down the trail is the junction with the spur trail leading off to the left toward the scenic lookout mentioned earlier. This 0.8-mile linear trail ends at a high point in the center of the loop formed by the Blue Trail and provides a good but limited view of the surrounding countryside. Back on the main train, the two loops soon split, with the Green Loop heading generally westward back toward the trailhead, 1.1 miles from this fork in the trail. About 0.8 mile from the end of the trail, hikers will pass the junction with the Black Trail feeding in from the left. From here it's only 0.3 mile back to the trailhead.

To reach the Blue Loop, hikers must first hike the outward, or northern, leg of the Green Loop past the spur trail leading to the scenic lookout, heading south to the fork in the trail. Here hikers will take the left fork and head southeast for nearly 1 mile. About 0.35 mile along this leg of the trail, hikers will pass the junction with the outbound leg of the Black Loop that heads south from this point. From this junction the pathway continues east for 0.65 mile before swinging north. The trail continues toward Lake Michigan for 0.4 mile before turning west for the 1-mile hike back to the junction of the two loops. Here hikers have two options: Head back to the trailhead by backtracking along the northern leg of the Green Loop; or retrace the 0.2 mile of trail shared by the two loops, then follow the southern leg of the Green Loop back to the trailhead. Either way, hikers will have to use the first loop to get back to the trailhead.

The final loop is another 2.5-mile trail system that features more hills and valleys to be negotiated. It is a less difficult task for hikers than skiers but challenging nonetheless. To reach the start of the Black Loop, hikers must first trace the first half of the Green Loop, the shared pathway, and 0.35 mile of the southern leg of the Blue Loop. Once at the junction, hikers head south for 0.9 mile, turn west for another 0.9 mile, and then go north for 0.6 mile to a junction with the return leg of the Green Trail leading back to the trailhead.

Key points:

1.25 Junction with the Blue Loop

1.4 Spur trail to high-ground lookout

Note: The three loops are each 2.5 miles long; following them requires only an eye to watching the color-coded trail markers.

30 Dunes Hiking Trails

Highlights: A two-part loop system: an easy loop for the less adventurous and a challenging loop for hikers willing to climb Sleeping Bear's tall sand dunes.

Type of hike: Linear and loop hikes.

Total distance: 6.8 miles.

Difficulty: Moderate to strenuous.

Best months: August through October.

Maps: USGS Glen Haven; National Park Service Dunes Hiking Trail map.

Permits and fees: Sleeping Bear Dunes Park Pass: $7.00 for 7 days; $15.00 for 12

months (from date of purchase, not a calendar year). Camping is available at D. H. Day Campground for $10 per night.

Special considerations: Dune climb at the start of the point-to-point Dunes Trail; Maritime Museum at Sleeping Bear Point.

For more information: Sleeping Bear Dunes Lakeshore, 9922 Front Street, Empire, MI 49630-9797; headquarters and visitor information, (231) 326-5134.

Parking and trailhead facilities: Parking is adequate at both trailheads.

Finding the trailhead: From Empire drive north 6 miles on Michigan Highway 109. The Dune Climb trailhead is on the left and is well marked. The loop trailhead is adjacent to the Maritime Museum off Michigan Highway 209. To reach the trailhead, continue north on M–109 to the junction with M–209. Follow M–209 for about 1.5 miles to the museum and trailhead.

The hikes:

The Dune Climb–Dunes Trail is a point-to-point hike of nearly 4 miles that requires at least four hours to complete. The 2.8-mile loop at Sleeping Bear Point is a relaxing hike through much the same habitat but without the dramatic changes in elevations.

The **Dunes Trail** is the most popular of all the trail systems in Sleeping Bear National Lakeshore because of the nearly 150-foot **Dune Climb** at the start of the point-to-point trail. There are few trees here, but the grasses, wildflowers, and occasional windswept tree make this a starkly beautiful area. The sandy shoreline of Lake Michigan and the panorama of the dunes environment make this an unforgettable hike.

The trail begins only a few yards from the parking lot off M–109, which is probably the last solid footing you will have for the next four hours. Ascending the dune in front of you will test your resolve and remind you that you have knees and thigh muscles in need of conditioning. Take your time climbing the dune, because you have a long way to go; even though the next few dunes don't demand the same kind of climb, they will still be taxing.

The top of this first dune rises about 890 feet above sea level. From there the first of the blue trail markers will be visible, as will the next dune to conquer. Atop

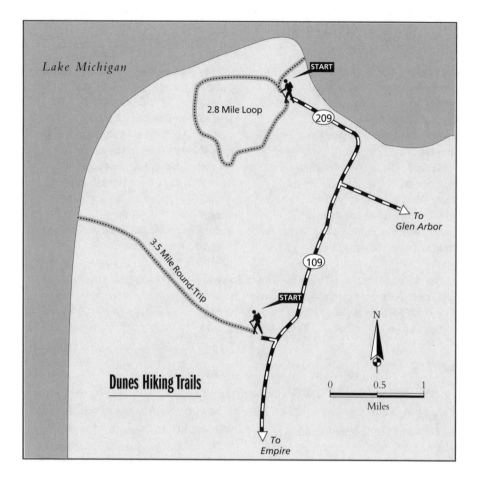

Lake Michigan

START

2.8 Mile Loop

209

To
Glen Arbor

3.5 Mile Round-Trip

109

START

N

Dunes Hiking Trails

0   0.5   1
Miles

To
Empire

the next dune hikers get their first look at the welcome waters of Lake Michigan, still a ways off. The trail signpost indicates 1 mile to go, but there are a few climbs left before you can cool your feet in the lake. In this dune environment, the only things to break the monotony of sand are patches of tough beach grass. The footing is tough.

From the last big dune, hikers will get a treat: a view of South Manitou Island with its historic lighthouse. From the top of this last tall dune, it's only about 0.5 mile to the shore of Lake Michigan. The trail offers no loops back to the trailhead, so you must retrace your steps.

The **loop trail at Sleeping Bear Point** is a more leisurely walk through the sandy environment that has made Sleeping Bear Dunes National Lakeshore such a popular stop for tourists and hikers. The trail is well marked and offers no real challenge for even the casual hiker, although it is still a sandy trail and walking can be tough on poorly protected feet. Vegetation is not quite as sparse as on the Dune Climb Trail, but it still isn't sufficient to provide a lot of solid footing.

Springtime in this corner of the system can be picturesque, since wildflowers tough enough to survive the windswept nature of the area provide a colorful backdrop for the stark sand dunes.

Key points:

0.1 150-foot dune climb at start of the Dunes Trail

31 Shauger Hill Hiking Trail

Highlights: A wander through beech and maple forests, open fields and meadows, and pine plantations. The trail does not afford a view of Sleeping Bear's lakeshore sand dunes.
Type of hike: Loop hike.
Total distance: 2.4 miles.
Difficulty: Moderate.
Best months: August through October.
Map: National Park Service Shauger Hill Hiking Trail map.
Permits and fees: Sleeping Bear Dunes Park Pass: $7.00 for 7 days; $15.00 for 12 months (from date of purchase, not a

calendar year). Camping is available at D. H. Day Campground for $10 per night.
Special considerations: A nonshoreline trail touring the forest that holds the dunes in place.
For more information: Sleeping Bear Dunes Lakeshore, 9922 Front Street, Empire, MI 49630-9797; headquarters, (231) 326-5134; visitor information, (231) 326-5134.
Parking and trailhead facilities: Adequate parking is available at the trailhead.

Finding the trailhead: From Empire drive north on Michigan Highway 109 for 3.5 miles to the junction with Scenic Drive. The trailhead and parking area are about 0.5 mile from the junction.

The hike:

The Shauger Hill Hiking Trail is one of the few trails in the park that don't provide a view of the famous dunes that give the region its name. This inland trail loop provides a look at the "other" side of the dunes area: the forests that hold it all in place along the Lake Michigan shoreline.

Hikers set out from the trailhead in a southerly direction, heading clockwise to cross Scenic Drive in just a few yards. The next landmark is the crossing of Shauger

Hill Road. From here it's on into the beech-and-maple forest that dominates the landscape.

The trail winds through the forested area for nearly a mile before crossing Shauger Hill Road for the last time as the trail turns back north for the final 1.4 miles to the trailhead. The trail is well marked and easy to follow as it snakes its way back to the start point. There are a number of steep downhill stretches along this segment of the trail, so take your time as you head back to the car.

The final 200 yards of the loop are reached after the second crossing of Scenic Drive. From here it's an easy walk south back to the trailhead. Although not long, Shauger Hill Hiking Trail offers a different perspective on Sleeping Bear Dunes National Lakeshore. Plan on including this hike in a day's adventuring in the region.

Key points:

Few landmarks highlight this trail, but it is easy to follow.

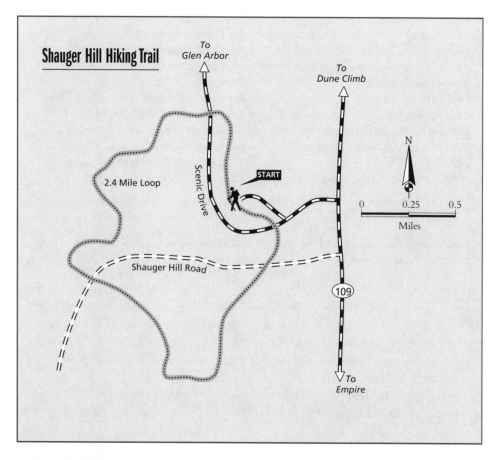

32 Windy Moraine Loop

Highlights: A short, easy hike to a mix of shoreline and upland habitats.
Type of hike: Loop hike.
Total distance: 1.5 miles.
Difficulty: Easy.
Best months: August through October.
Map: National Park Service area map.
Permits and fees: Sleeping Bear Dunes Park Pass: $7.00 for 7 days; $15.00 for 12 months (from date of purchase, not a calen-dar year). Camping is available at D. H. Day Campground for $10 per night.
Special considerations: Scenic vistas of the Lake Michigan shoreline.
For more information: Sleeping Bear Dunes Lakeshore, 9922 Front Street, Empire, MI 49630-9797; headquarters, (231) 326-5134; visitor information, (231) 326-5134.
Parking and trailhead facilities: Parking is adequate at the trailhead.

Finding the trailhead: From Empire drive north on Michigan Highway 109 for 4 miles to the junction with Welch Road. Turn right for the final 200-yard drive to the trailhead.

The hike:

This loop is a short and easy excursion but is meant to be combined with the other trails in the Sleeping Bear Dunes National Lakeshore area to create a longer stay in this scenic portion of the Lower Peninsula. The trail makes a great diversion from the sandy loops nearer the Lake Michigan shoreline and provides unique photo opportunities.

The first 0.75 mile will expose hikers to a rich diversity of habitats, both naturally occurring and man-made. Fields, forests, and buffer zones all are present along this half of the loop. Remnants of an old farm are marked by a few remaining apple trees. About 0.25 mile from the trailhead, you will find the decaying reminder that a sawmill once operated here: decomposing slab wood, which feeds a whole community of forest life. About 0.5 mile from the trailhead, a large sugar maple provides a welcome respite from the heat of summer. It's a comfortable spot to reflect on whatever is on your mind.

From this point on to Windy Moraine Overlook, be on the lookout for wildlife of all sorts, including squirrels, raccoons, and even deer. The Windy Moraine Overlook is the halfway point in the loop; from here you will be able to see a large portion of the Sleeping Bear Dunes National Lakeshore.

From the overlook the trail heads north and then west back toward the trailhead. The final landmark is a pine plantation about 0.25 mile from the end of the trail.

Key points:

0.25 Old Sawmill
0.75 Windy Moraine Overlook

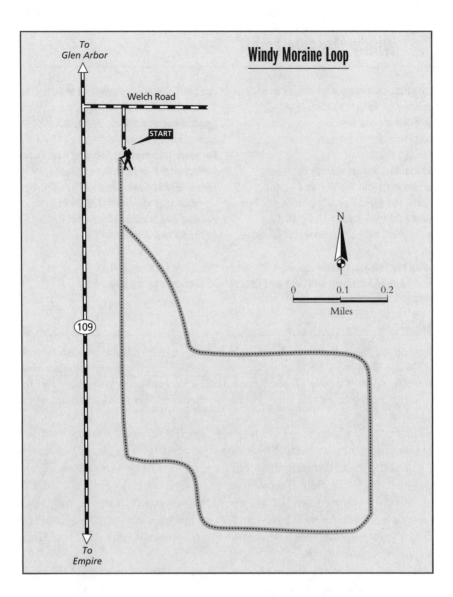

To
Glen Arbor

Windy Moraine Loop

Welch Road

START

109

N

0   0.1   0.2

Miles

To
Empire

33 Old Indian Trails

Highlights: The two loops of this trail system trace the crests of ancient tree-covered dunes that once marked the postglacial shoreline in the region. The trail was used by local Native Americans to reach the lake to fish and camp.
Type of hike: Loop hike.
Total distance: 4.55 miles.
Difficulty: Easy.
Best months: July through October.
Maps: USGS Frankfort; National Park Service Old Indian Trail map.
Permits and fees: Sleeping Bear Dunes Park

Pass: $7.00 for 7 days; $15.00 for 12 months (from date of purchase, not a calendar year). Camping is available at D. H. Day Campground for $10 per night.
Special considerations: Isolated beaches and carpets of seasonal wildflowers.
For more information: Sleeping Bear Dunes Lakeshore, 9922 Front Street, Empire, MI 49630-9797; headquarters, (231) 326-5134; visitor information, (231) 326-5134.
Parking and trailhead facilities: Adequate parking at the trailhead.

Finding the trailhead: The trailhead is approximately 12 miles south of the park's visitor center on Michigan Highway 22. If approaching from Frankfort (north), the entrance is just past the M-22–Sutter Road junction, on the left.

The hike:

The two loops of this trail follow the crests of ancient tree-covered dunes, well inland from today's shoreline. The dunes mark the postglacial shoreline of Lake Michigan. The mix of hardwoods and pines that cover the area provide welcome relief from summer heat.

Once out of the parking lot at the trailhead, hikers are swallowed up by the hardwood and pine forest that covers much of the first sections of the trail. You will pass a junction with the return leg of the trail about 150 yards from the trailhead. Continue north past the junction with the middle trail to a point 0.3 mile from the start point, where the trail takes a decidedly westward tack.

For the next 1.2 miles you will work your way over a series of low dunes covered with vegetation and pass through beech, maple, and oak forest. A few low-lying wet areas break the tree cover, but for the most part you will remain in the forest until you break out onto the beach.

At the end of the westward leg you will reach a marker indicating the path to the shoreline of Platte Bay. The short spur is only 0.3 mile long, but the sandy trail here makes hiking more difficult. Once at the lakeshore you will be able to see both North and South Manitou Islands, the famous Sleeping Bear Dune, and miles of unspoiled beaches to the east.

Returning to the junction, head southeast past the junction with the middle trail for nearly 0.25 mile to where the return leg of the Old Indian Trail heads easterly. The trek back to the trailhead is about 0.75 mile.

The center, or middle, trail splits the outer loop through the middle of the wooded area surrounding this system. It provides an interesting diversion. Take it, then turn right at the junction with the outbound leg. You will reach the trailhead in just a matter of minutes.

Key points:

1.6 Spur trail to Platte Bay—0.3 mile to beach

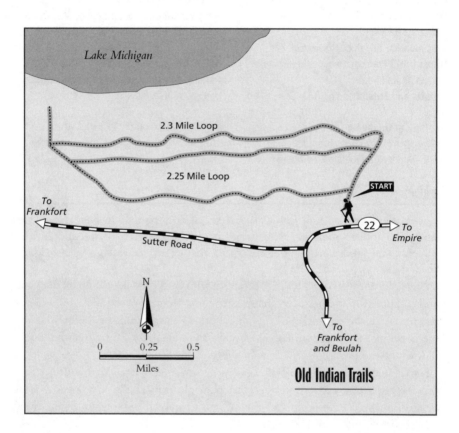

34 Empire Bluff Trail

Highlights: A picturesque hike with a final panorama that has caused many hikers to turn a one-hour hike into an all-day reflection on the beauty of Lake Michigan, spread out at the foot of a 400-foot-tall sand dune.

Type of hike: Linear hike.

Total distance: 2 miles.

Difficulty: Moderate.

Best months: July through October.

Maps: USGS Empire; National Park Service Empire Bluff Trail map.

Permits and fees: Sleeping Bear Dunes Park Pass: $7.00 for 7 days; $15.00 for 12

months (from date of purchase, not a calendar year). Camping is available at D. H. Day Campground for $10 per night.

Special considerations: Six interpretive stations and a blend of natural and man-made regional history.

For more information: Sleeping Bear Dunes Lakeshore, 9922 Front Street, Empire, MI 49630-9797; headquarters, (231) 326-5134; visitor information, (231) 326-5134.

Parking and trailhead facilities: There is adequate parking at the trailhead.

Finding the trailhead: Drive south from the park's visitor center on Michigan Highway 22 for 2 miles to the junction with Wilco Road; turn left. The trailhead is 1 mile down the road, on the left.

The hike:

Empire Bluff is rated by many as the best 2-mile hike anywhere in the state of Michigan. The hike is not difficult, and the rewards along the route are similar to those reserved for hikers who endure much more difficult systems. The hike is

Old-growth hardwoods host a variety of wildlife and flowers, including the trillium.

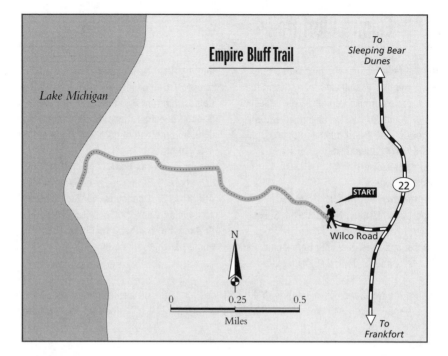

Empire Bluff Trail

Lake Michigan

To Sleeping Bear Dunes

START

22

Wilco Road

N

0   0.25   0.5

Miles

To Frankfort

interrupted by six interpretive stations and a spectacular view at the outer end of the trail, revealing much of Sleeping Bear Dunes National Lakeshore, Platte Bay, and, 7 miles offshore, South Manitou Island.

Hikers get a taste of hilly terrain right from the start. A boulder left behind by a receding glacier some 12,000 years ago marks the first of the six interpretive sites. From here hikers will pass through open fields and past farm equipment left behind from an era long gone by. The soils weren't rich enough to support many crops, but hay farmers eked out a living from this area until about the mid-1940s. Leaving the fields, hikers move into a mature beech-and-maple forest. The trail here is fairly level. During summer hikers will enjoy the shade of the forest and a sprinkling of wild-flowers.

The hilly nature of the Empire Bluff Trail reappears once again as hikers move into an area called the Old Orchard. This isn't actually an orchard, but there is a grove of fruit trees here, which may have grown from fruit discarded in the area. The remains of small American yew, once plentiful in the area, are the focus of Interpretive Site 5, the lead-in for the spectacular vista waiting just ahead.

A short climb to Site 6 and the Empire Bluff Overlook reveals a breathtaking view of the park and its miles of shoreline. The trail swings south, following a board-walk for 500 feet to an observation deck.

Hikers will want to spend time at the vista, and then will have to retrace their steps to the trailhead.

Key points:

The outward hike ends with a spectacular view of the park and the Lake Michigan shoreline.

35 Platte Plains Trails

Highlights: Dune scenery is the highlight of this loop.

Type of hike: Loop hike.

Total distance: 13 miles.

Difficulty: Easy.

Best months: July through October.

Maps: USGS Beulah; National Park Service Platte Plains Trail map.

Permits and fees: Sleeping Bear Dunes Park Pass: $7.00 for 7 days; $15.00 for 12 months (from date of purchase, not a calen-dar year). Camping is available at D. H. Day Campground for $10 per night.

Special considerations: Scenic overlooks along Lake Michigan shoreline.

For more information: Sleeping Bear Dunes Lakeshore, 9922 Front Street, Empire, MI 49630-9797; headquarters, (231) 326-5134; visitor information, (231) 326-5134.

Parking and trailhead facilities: There is adequate parking at the trailhead.

Finding the trailhead: To reach the north trailhead, drive south from Empire on Michigan Highway 22 for 3.5 miles until you reach Esch Road. Turn right; the trailhead is 1 mile from the junction. To reach the central trailhead, drive south 1.5 miles for the Esch Road junction and watch for signs on the right directing you to Trails End Road. The trailhead is 0.5 mile from the turn. The southern trailhead is in the Platte River Campground. Drive south from the Trails End Road junction for 4 miles to Lake Michigan Road. Turn right and follow the signs to the campground, on the right.

The hike:

The Platte River Campground is a popular stop for summer users of the Sleeping Bear Dunes area, but few venture out on the trails, leaving hikers a bit of solitude and the beauty of the Lake Michigan shoreline. This trail system also has a remote wilderness campground, with no water, sources of food, or heavy foot-traffic to spoil your adventure. The loops of the trail system allow for plenty of time to explore the varied environments found along these trails. Lakes, streams, and the full range of dry habitats make a visit to the Platte Plains Trail a constantly changing adventure.

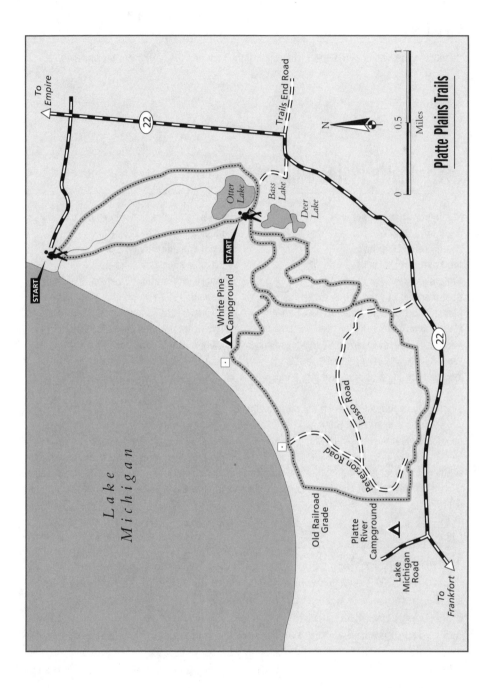

Lake Michigan

START

To Empire

22

Trails End Road

N

Platte Plains Trails

0.5   1

0   Miles

Otter Lake

Bass Lake

Deer Lake

START

White Pine Campground

Lasso Road

Peterson Road

Old Railroad Grade

Platte River Campground

Lake Michigan Road

To Frankfort

22

Leaving the Platte River Campground (the southern trailhead), hikers enter a pine thicket that masks rolling terrain. The trees open up on sand dunes along the shoreline of Lake Michigan about 0.5 mile from the trailhead. The soft, sandy trail makes walking a little strenuous, but it ends soon, so just slow down a bit.

From a junction with the first of three trails to scenic overlooks, the trail turns east and begins to parallel the shoreline, crossing Peterson Road in 0.5 mile. A second scenic overlook can be reached by turning left onto Peterson Road and hiking a few hundred yards to the lake. It is about 1 mile from the Peterson Road crossing to the final overlook site; hikers will pass through mixed hardwoods and pine.

Beyond the third overlook, after nearly 1 mile of gently rolling terrain, hikers reach the remote White Pine Campground. The campground is set between wooded ridges and contains only six sites. Everything you need will have to be carried in and out of this beautiful little campsite.

From the campground, the loop continues southeast for 0.8 mile to the first junction with the 3.6-mile loop. The trail takes a decidedly southern tack, making a 1.1-mile leg to the southern junction with the smallest loop in the Platte Plains system. About 0.3 mile past this junction, hikers cross Lasso Road, continuing west for a 2-mile trek back to the second crossing of Peterson Road. Hikers continue west, then turn north for the 0.3-mile hike to a signpost that will direct you back to the Platte River Campground.

The shortest loop, which connects the trailhead from Trails End Road (the central trailhead) with the main loop, shares 1.1 miles of the bigger loop's eastern leg. The trail meanders through wooded and wet areas, eventually following a portion of the western shoreline of Deer Lake before returning to the Trails End Road trailhead.

The 4.5-mile loop from Esch Road can also be started at the Trails End Road entry point. This trail loop follows a course around Otter Lake, then follows the course of Otter Creek to Lake Michigan and back again. This wet section of trail presents the problem of keeping feet dry, but the variety of wildlife found in this area will distract you from sodden feet.

Key points:

0.5   Lake Michigan shoreline

2.25   White Pine Campground

7.5   Platte River Campground

36 Ocqueoc Falls Bicentennial Pathway

Highlights: The trail shadows one of northern Michigan's finest steelhead and salmon rivers and offers a view of the largest waterfall in the Lower Peninsula.

Type of hike: Loop hike.

Total distance: 14 miles.

Difficulty: Moderate.

Best months: July through September.

Map: Department of Natural Resources trail map; the trail is well marked with blue blazes and signposts.

Permits and fees: None.

Special considerations: The trail system is used by fishing and hunting enthusiasts starting in early fall, so dress in bright colors.

For more information: Rogers City Chamber of Commerce, 292 South Bradley Highway, Rogers City, MI 49779; (989) 734-2535 or (800) 622-4148; Department of Natural Resources, P.O. Box 667, Gaylord, MI 49735; (989) 732-3541.

Parking and trailhead facilities: Parking is adequate. There are pit toilets available and nearby well for drinking water.

Finding the trailhead: The trailhead is 11 miles west of Rogers City off Michigan Highway 68. Signs will direct you the remaining 400 yards to the parking lot off Ocqueoc Falls Road. It is well marked. A map board at the trailhead outlines the trail loops, and there is usually a large supply of maps in a holder below the board.

The hike:

The Ocqueoc Falls Bicentennial Pathway offers three loops through terrain bordering one of northeast Michigan's premier steelhead and salmon streams.

The shortest of the three loops is 3 miles and caters to the casual hiker with only moderate changes in elevation. The 5-mile and 6-mile loops share the same route but extend farther along the Ocqueoc River through some very sandy and hilly terrain. An added difficulty is the remoteness of the outer legs of the first two loops and the entire third loop north of the Little Ocqueoc River. A good pair of boots are recommended to compensate for the variety of trail surfaces. Limestone outcroppings along the river are particularly hard on ill-shod hikers.

Ocqueoc Falls, created by a series of limestone escarpments, are the largest falls in the Lower Peninsula. The mix of highland hardwoods and pines here blend with cedar bogs and swamps along the trail to create a tapestry of color, particularly in fall. Wildlife abounds along the trail, including deer, wild turkey, small game, and a variety of waterfowl. Be alert to the presence of black bear, particularly on the longer loops.

The first two loops of the system are south of the Little Ocqueoc River. Almost immediately after leaving the trailhead, hikers start to climb—a pattern that will become familiar on the outbound legs of the first loop. The climb up sandy, well-marked trails carries hikers into the hardwood highlands of the area.

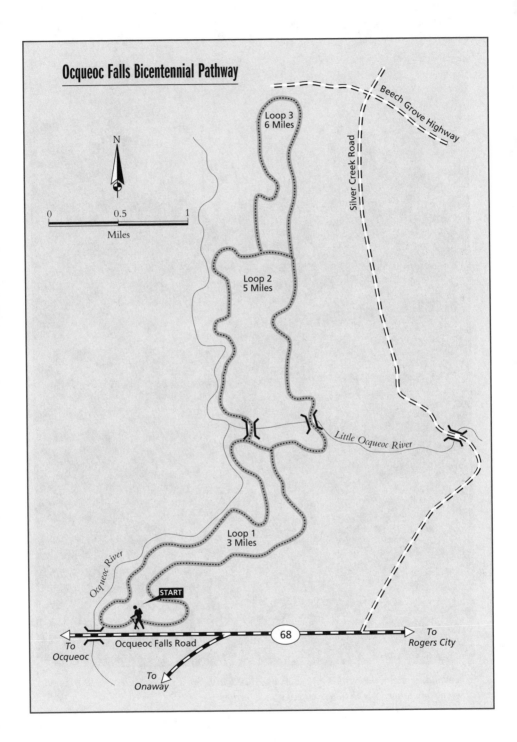

Ocqueoc Falls Bicentennial Pathway

N

0   0.5   1
Miles

Loop 3
6 Miles

Loop 2
5 Miles

Little Ocqueoc River

Silver Creek Road

Beech Grove Hwy

Loop 1
3 Miles

Ocqueoc River

START

To
Ocqueoc

Ocqueoc Falls Road

68

To
Rogers City

To
Onaway

Snow and ice frame the scenic Ocqueoc Falls. Although the area remains accessible year-round, the trails are impassable to hikers once the snow arrives.

The next 1.5 miles go through a mixed forest of hardwoods and conifers and lead to the junction with the shorter second loop. Hikers looking for the complete tour often combine the first two loops into a 5-mile hike by taking the connector trail to the left for the 100-yard hike toward the river and then, instead of turning left to head back to the trailhead, turning right to hike the 2-mile loop in reverse.

From the junction with the return leg of the first loop, head north for a brief look at the Ocqueoc River before reaching the footbridge over the Little Ocqueoc River that leads to the final, 3-mile loop in the system. To complete the first loop, follow the trail along the south bank of the Little Ocqueoc as it climbs back into the hardwood highlands for the return trip to the earlier junction with the second loop. You will have to retrace the short connector leg of the 3-mile loop, dropping down from the ridges to shadow the Ocqueoc River back to the trailhead.

The 1.5 miles back to the parking lot are a mix of sandy and sometimes rocky trail surfaces. The river will be a constant reminder that you are on

Morel hunters find plenty of the tasty mushrooms near the banks of the Ocqueoc River and in the stands of mature hardwoods lining the waterway.

the right track as you head back to the starting point. About 200 yards from the end of this loop, you will reach the base of Ocqueoc Falls. The limestone escarpment is not a dramatic change in elevation, but a series of drops of 3 to 5 feet gather momentum along a series of deep pools. From the falls, it's an easy climb up to the parking lot. There is a picnic area at the top of the hill along with pit toilets.

Hikers who want to travel the last loop in the Bicentennial Pathway will have to return to the footbridge over the Little Ocqueoc River. Its trailhead is reached only after hiking the first loops and is an add-on for hikers with the time and energy to complete the extra 3 miles. This section of the trail is also rated moderate, due more to the remoteness than trail difficulty. The terrain of this outer loop is similar to that of the first two. The outbound leg climbs onto the hardwood ridges before dropping back down to trace the course of the Ocqueoc River to its junction with the Little Ocqueoc. From the junction of the two rivers, hikers should turn east and return to the footbridge for the trek back to the trailhead at the parking lot.

One note of caution for hikers visiting the trail after September 15: The areas along both banks of the two rivers are very popular with both big- and small-game hunters. Anyone hiking these trails at that time should wear bright-colored clothing and avoid straying off established pathways. The segments of trail that shoulder on the Ocqueoc River are high-traffic pathways during early fall when salmon enter the stream, providing an extra distraction for hikers. In early spring, low-lying areas that trace the river may be a bit wet, requiring a detour or two, but will still be passable.

Key points:

0.5 Ocqueoc Falls, west of the parking lot

1.55 First footbridge over the Little Ocqueoc River

5.7 Second footbridge over the Little Ocqueoc River

37 Hoist Lakes Foot Travel Area

Highlights: Small lakes, wetlands, upland hardwood ridges, bluffs, steep hills, and conifer forests in the heart of the Huron National Forest.

Type of hike: Loop hike.

Total distance: 21 miles.

Difficulty: Moderate to challenging.

Best months: July through September.

Maps: USGS Curran and Bucks Pond; Huron National Forest Hoist Lakes Foot Travel Area map.

Permits and fees: None.

Special considerations: The area is used extensively by small- and big-game hunters starting in late September and throughout the rest of the fall hunting season. Plan your hike accordingly, and wear brightly colored clothing. No mountain bikes or other mechanized trail use allowed.

For more information: District Ranger, U.S. Forest Service, Huron National Forest, Harrisville Ranger District, Harrisville, MI 48740; (989) 724-5431.

Parking and trailhead facilities: Parking in the small gravel parking lot is usually adequate, but it may get crowded later in the fall.

Finding the trailhead: To reach the start point for the west loop, drive north of Glennie on Michigan Highway 65 for 5 miles to Au Sable Road. Then drive north for 3 miles to the West Loop trailhead. To reach the East Loop trailhead, drive north of Glennie on M-65 for 7 miles, or from Harrisville drive west on Michigan Highway 72 for 22 miles to the M-65 junction. Turn south on M-65 for the 0.5-mile drive to the trailhead.

The hikes:

The Hoist Lakes area is managed specifically for enjoyment by hikers and other non-mechanized visitors. Mountain bikers are prohibited from the area. The area's nearly 11,000 acres are located in the heart of Huron National Forest, offering foot travelers an opportunity to get away from the hectic pace of city life; the trails are just a short drive from urban sprawl.

The environment in this corner of the northeast Lower Peninsula includes small lakes, wetlands, upland hardwood ridges, bluffs, and steep hills, plus extensive conifer forests. Resident wildlife includes Michigan's "black ghost," the always-there but seldom-seen black bear. The 20 miles of trails are challenging, punctuated by hills topping out at more than 1,000 feet. This is as close as many hikers will ever get to genuine wilderness. The Hoist Lakes area is scenic, tranquil, and easily accessible. Trails are well marked and solid underfoot, but several hills increase the physical challenge.

The shorter **west loop** is hilly and provides access to the best fishing lakes in the area. From the parking lot, the trail heads east into the area to join with the loop about 0.5 mile away. The hike is relatively easy at first, which is somewhat deceiving because the terrain doesn't remain easy for long. At the loop junction, hikers have

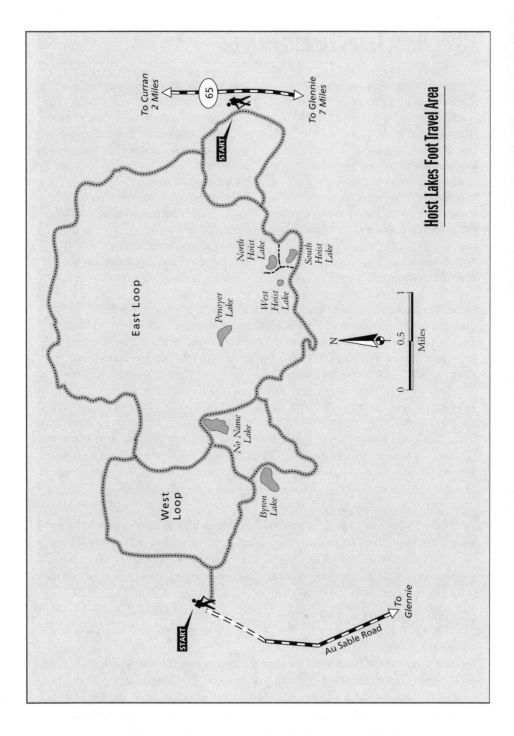

Hoist Lakes Foot Travel Area

The habitat in the Hoist Lakes Foot Travel Area changes suddenly from wetlands to dry hardwood hilltops as hikers move through the area.

the option of turning south for the trek to Byron Lake or starting the clockwise trace of the 8-mile west loop.

The clockwise hike starts out on an ill-marked trail leg that's a bit confusing but eventually becomes clear as you move away from the junction. It is a 2.25-mile trek to the next junction in the loop, the first contact with the east loop. This is a hilly, sometimes steep section of the trail but should pose no problem for hikers who have time to proceed slowly. Hikers find themselves ridge-hopping before reaching Post 11 and their first look at No Name Lake. The east and west loops share the next 2.5 miles of the system, as hikers move between Marker Posts 5 and 12. The trail skirts the northern and eastern shores of the lake before turning south for the final 1.25 miles of the shared trail to post 12.

There is a major climb for hikers heading toward Byron Lake, a steep ascent that puts hikers at nearly 1,200 feet and provides a great view of the area. From the ridgeline, hikers descend slightly to make the final 0.5-mile trek to the eastern shore of Byron Lake. The trail soon passes Post 10 and then 9, along with markers for designated campsites near the lake. From the lake, hikers head west to the junction with the short trail spur to the trailhead and the parking lot.

Hiking the **east loop** can be done in either direction depending on how much time you have to reach a designated campsite. If time permits, hike the trail in a counterclockwise direction; if finding a campsite is higher on your agenda, head west toward Hoist Lakes campsites, about 2.5 miles away. Either way, the trail is generally easy to follow.

Hikers heading to the right from the trailhead will have a fairly easy trek for the first 5 miles as the trail traces through cutover areas and along portions of old logging roads. The path meanders through the eastern and northern sections of the Hoist Lakes Foot Travel Area, probably the easiest sections of the trail system to hike. As hikers reach Junction Post 5, the point at which the two loops in this system share a length of trail, the terrain begins to change a bit, becoming hilly and a struggle for those who made the long trip "around the top" from the trailhead.

Past Junction Post 12, hikers will make the left turn to head for the 2-plus-mile trek to the area's namesakes, the Hoist Lakes. At Junction Post 13, a spur trail leads to established campsites around North and South Hoist Lakes. These campsites are less than 0.5 mile north of the main trail and are not difficult to locate.

The final leg of the east loop, a 1-mile span to Junction Post 14 and the final 1.5 miles to the trailhead and the parking lot, is a mix of representative habitats found throughout the Hoist Lakes area. Hills—one a climb of more than 1,000 feet—and wet marshes are strung together along this section of the pathway. More than one hiker has compared this final leg of the journey to "a final reminder of what we've gone through for the first 9 miles!"

The closer hikers are to parking lots and trailheads, the more the chance of encountering hunters during fall months, particularly from September 15 through late November.

Key points:

The mix of moist and upland habitats requires good footwear and a determination to finish a loop once it's started.

38 Rifle River Recreation Area

Highlights: A quiet getaway nestled in the heart of the Au Sable State Forest that's perfect for hikers looking for a mix of terrain, scenery, and trails the entire family can handle.

Type of hike: Loop hike.

Total distance: 13 miles.

Difficulty: Easy to moderate.

Best months: July through September.

Maps: USGS Rose City and Selkirk; Department of Natural Resources area brochure.

Permits and fees: Modern campsites, $15.00 per day; rustic campsites, $9.00 per day. State park daily vehicle pass, $4.00; annual pass, $20.00.

Special considerations: The area is used by small- and big-game hunters throughout the fall, so wear brightly colored clothing if you visit the area in autumn.

For more information: Rifle River Recreation Area, 2550 East Rose City Road, Lupton, MI 48635; (989) 473-2258.

Parking and trailhead facilities: There is adequate parking at the trailheads, but the best is reserved for campers adjacent to the campsites. Water is available; other amenities and services are limited.

Finding the trailhead: The area is 15 miles southwest of West Branch and 4.75 miles east of Rose City, off County Road F-28. Trailheads for this system are located in the campgrounds on Grousehaven and Jewett Lakes. The Grousehaven Lake trailhead provides access to the short loop east of the lake, as well as the longer southern loop. The Jewett Lake trailhead intersects the longer southern loop between Jewett and Devoe Lakes. Both trailheads/campgrounds are off Ranch Road.

The hike:

The Rifle River Recreation Area is a multiuse area. Once a private hunting and fishing retreat owned by the late H. M. Jewett, the area became the property of the state of Michigan in 1945. It was transferred to the Parks Division in 1963 and developed to the extent seen today.

The 4,300-acre recreation area blends nearly all the habitats and environments found in northern Michigan. Its overall beauty and solitude draw more than 100,000 visitors annually. The mix of habitat is of particular interest to birders and photographers. In the northern section of the area, hikers will encounter upland hardwood ridges and the steepest climbs in the system; the southern loop is a trek through a blend of dry uplands, lake, and river habitats. The area is a haven for hunters in pursuit of both large and small game, and fishing enthusiasts will find plenty of action in the ten lakes in the region.

Two main trailheads provide access to the trail system; there is also an access point in the picnic area on the north shore of Grousehaven Lake. Although you will miss the first 0.5 mile of the trail from the Grousehaven Lake Campground, it's from the picnic area that this hike description starts. Hikers will have little trouble

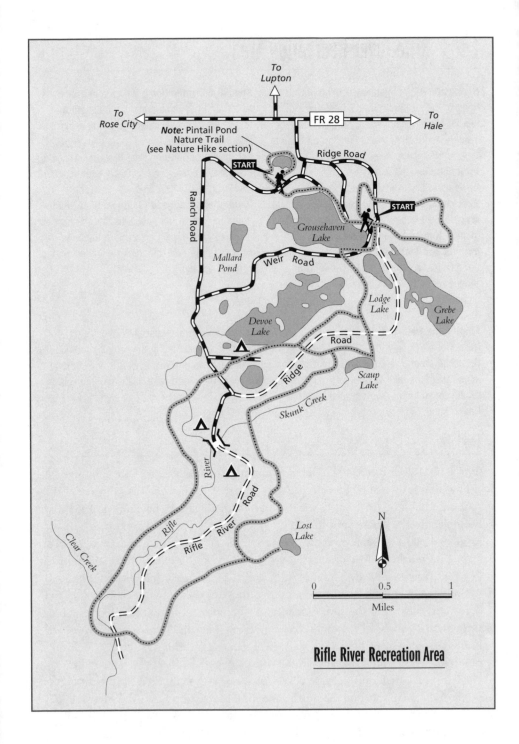

To Lupton

To Rose City

FR 28

To Hale

Note: Pintail Pond
Nature Trail
(see Nature Hike section)

START

Ridge Road

START

Ranch Road

Grousehaven
Lake

Weir Road

Mallard
Pond

Lodge
Lake

Grebe
Lake

Devoe
Lake

Road

Ridge

Scaup
Lake

Skunk Creek

River

Lost
Lake

Rifle

Rifle River Road

Clear Creek

N

0   0.5   1

Miles

Rifle River Recreation Area

Thick belts of conifers accent the stands of mature hardwoods in the area, providing a maze of habitats that attract a variety of wildlife.

following the first few hundred yards from the campground to this start point, but day hikers without campsites should use the picnic area.

Shortly after leaving the picnic area, hikers reach the junction with a 2-mile loop through a beautiful section of upland hardwood ridges. This hilly and often challenging loop also contains the highest point in the area, a 1,060-foot rise about one-third of the way around the loop. The ridge-hopping required for the climb to the high point becomes hill-dropping for the remainder of the loop as hikers head back to rejoin the main trail as it shadows Weir Road.

The main pathway generally follows the road and the shoreline of Grousehaven Lake as it heads south to the junction marker for a second loop trail that provides access to Scaup Lake or the short loop's western leg, which follows the shoreline of Devoe Lake. At the end of the Scaup Lake Loop, hikers head generally south along the largest loop in the area, a 6-mile trek that flanks, from a distance at times, the Rifle River.

Approximately 1 mile from the junction, a bridge provides access over Skunk Creek. This leg of the hike is not tough but can be distracting for hikers on the lookout for photo opportunities. About 1.5 miles farther down the trail, a marker on the left points the way to Lost Lake, about 0.5 mile to the east.

Returning to the main trail, hikers take a westerly heading before reaching the first of the bridges over the Rifle River, about 1.5 miles away. You will have to cross a small creek before reaching the larger river, but it should present no problem. The next waterway, Clear Creek, is only 0.5 mile down the trail. From here, for more than 2 miles, hikers head nearly due north to the second bridge over the Rifle River. This leads to rustic Ranch Campground. From the campground, hikers turn northeast for the final portions of this 6-mile loop.

Within 0.5 mile after leaving the campground, the trail crosses Ranch Road and enters a high-traffic area that feeds the Devoe Lake Campground and boat launches for Devoe and Jewett Lakes. This area is used heavily in summer, so be aware of vehicles along local roads. In another 0.5 mile, hikers rejoin the short loop between Scaup and Devoe Lakes, this time on the leg opposite the Scaup Lake Loop. A few hundred yards east on this leg, the trail reaches the northbound portion of the trail leading back to the picnic area.

Note: There is no camping allowed along the trail except in designated campgrounds. Be sure to check the park map for the locations of these sites, and plan your hike accordingly.

Key points:

Trail loops are well marked and easy to follow.

39 Proud Lake Recreation Area

Highlights: The 4,000-acre park offers a mix of habitats and environments for hikers and the opportunity to photograph a wide variety of wildlife. The trail system is very family friendly.

Type of hike: Loop hike.

Total distance: 21 miles.

Difficulty: Easy.

Best months: June through October.

Maps: USGS Milford; Department of Natural Resources area map and brochures.

Permits and fees: Modern campsites, $18 per night. State park daily vehicle pass, $4.00; annual pass, $20.00.

Special considerations: Park is open year-round, and the trails, depending on snowfall, can be hiked all year.

For more information: Proud Lake Recreation Area, 3500 Wixom Road, Milford, MI 48382; (248) 685-2433.

Parking and trailhead facilities: Parking is available at the trailhead, but parking in the campground area is reserved for campers only.

Finding the trailhead: Proud Lake Recreation Area is 3 miles southeast of Milford and 7 miles north of Interstate 96 from the Wixom exit. The recreation area is flanked by major roads including Interstate 75 and I-96.

Park headquarters is the main trailhead for all hikes in the area. Approaching from the south, take the Wixom exit off I-96 and drive north for 6 miles to the trailhead. From Milford drive east on Commerce Road to Duck Lake Road, then turn right and follow the road for 2 miles to the trailhead.

Ponds and impoundments in the Proud Lake Recreation Area attract a variety of migratory birds each spring and fall.

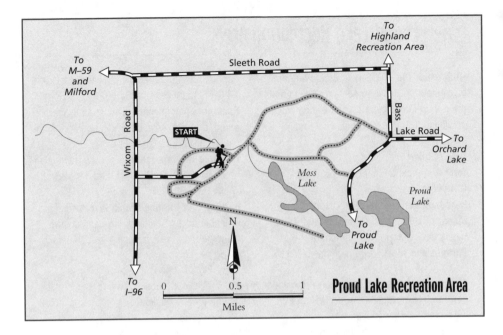

Proud Lake Recreation Area

The hike:

The Huron River Valley in metropolitan Oakland County provides the focal point for this major recreation area just minutes from downtown Detroit. The park was established in the mid-1940s and has changed very little in the interim. It continues to be one of the most utilized and most scenic of the state's recreation areas. The mix of environments provides a unique opportunity to view and photograph myriad species occupying everything from marshes, bogs, and other wetlands to meadows to upland forests that cover much of the area.

For hikers with fishing fever, the Huron River offers a great opportunity to catch rainbow and brown trout. The 3,614 acres of the Proud Lake Recreation Area afford blue-ribbon trout fishing. Weekend hikers will find more than enough to keep them busy: exploring nature trails, taking off on a cross-park excursion, or conveniently wandering along the river and wetting a line. Birders have the opportunity to visit nearly every type of ecosystem found in the state within the confines of the recreation area, and ponds and impoundments attract migratory birds each spring and fall.

The only real difficulty on any of the trails in the area is deciding where to go first. The pathways are easy to navigate and fairly easy to hike. The distance of the complete trail system, should you decide to hike it all in a single day, might boost the rating into the moderate category, but taken in moderation the system remains easy. Trails and loops from the trailhead at Park Headquarters offer paths into nearly every corner of the recreation area. Short loops that shadow the rivers and lakes of the area can be linked with longer loops along the outer edges of the park to create hikes to fit your needs and timetable. Contact Park Headquarters for the latest information on each of the pathways in the Proud Lake Recreation Area.

From the parking lot adjacent to headquarters, the trails fan out across the park, many first leading through the nature study area south of the Huron River. This first set of pathways can be used as the jumping-off point for most trails in the park. Trails that trace the eastern portions of the area can also be accessed from campgrounds along Proud Lake. Horseback trails in the western end of the park are separated from hiking trails to avoid conflicts. Trails are all clearly marked and easy to follow and present no special challenge to even the casual hiker.

Key points:

The only real difficulty is deciding which trail or area of the park to explore first. The trails are well marked and easy to follow.

40 Island Lake Recreation Area

Highlights: The 7 miles of river flanked by the park have been designated part of the National Scenic River Program, under the Natural Rivers Act. The terrain offers no special challenge; wildlife and scenery provide plenty of photographic opportunities.

Type of hike: Loop hike.

Total distance: 12 miles.

Difficulty: Easy.

Best months: June through October.

Map: An area map is available at Park Headquarters. Blue markers define trails, and pathways are covered by a layer of wood chips that leave little doubt as to which heading to take through the woods.

Permits and fees: Rustic campsites are available at no charge at press time. State park daily vehicle pass, $4.00; annual pass, $20.00.

Special considerations: The park attracts the attention of hunters, starting with early-season goose hunters and lasting through Michigan's deer season. If you hike in the fall, wear brightly colored clothing.

For more information: Island Lake Recreation Area, 12950 East Grand River, Brighton, MI 48116; (810) 229-7067.

Parking and trailhead facilities: Parking is available at the trailhead, but the area may be crowded once hunting season opens.

Finding the trailhead: The start point for the two loops in the park is the Riverbend Picnic Area. To reach the trailhead, drive 3 miles west of Brighton on Grand River Road to the intersection with Kensington Road. Turn right onto Kensington Road to the access road leading to the picnic area and the trailhead.

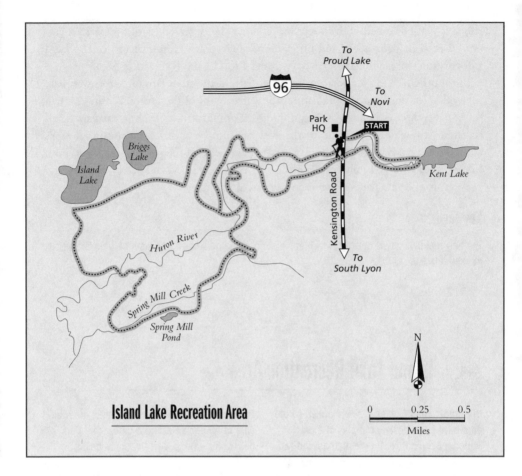

Island Lake Recreation Area

The hike:

With its proximity to the Detroit metro area, Island Lake Recreation Area is a convenient getaway from urban sprawl. The park offers two loop trails totaling 12 miles along the flanks of the scenic Huron River. The natural beauty of the riverline habitat makes this trail system one of the most popular in the region. The terrain provides no special challenge to casual hikers, but the beauty of the area gives plenty of reasons to stop and enjoy the scenery. Camping is available within the park boundaries for those who wish to extend their visit. The two loops in the park, although lengthy, are not at all difficult, so first-time or family hikers who have the time can easily complete either or both of them.

The **5-mile loop** that closely follows the course of the Huron River is the most scenic hike through the recreation area. It starts at the Riverbend Picnic Area, beginning in a clockwise direction and crossing the Huron River via an old cement bridge just yards from the trailhead. From the bridge it's just 0.2 mile to the junc-

Hikers will discover a variety of wildlife in the area, from Michigan's white-tailed deer to the small ground-dwelling red squirrel.

tion with the inbound leg of the larger Island Lake Loop. Stay to the right on the River Loop. From the junction, the trail heads north for nearly 0.7 mile before heading to the east and the trek to Kensington Road. For the next mile, hikers will make several slight climbs and corresponding descents as they move through the shade of mature hardwoods. About 2.5 miles from the trailhead, hikers will reach Kensington Road. Use the road bridge over the Huron River to start the return trip along the river. For the next mile the trail shadows the Huron, bending away for 1.3 miles before returning to the bank of the river for the rest of the hike back to the trailhead at Riverbend.

The longer **Island Lake Loop** starts behind the rest rooms at the picnic area. The trail's first landmark appears quickly: hikers must pass under a railroad bridge before reaching the northern bank of Spring Mill Creek. The pathway turns west along the creek and crosses the creek about 0.5 mile later. Hikers can use a bridge to reach the other side. The trail to this point is flat, but hilly terrain appears just beyond Spring Mill Pond. There are several steep hills along this stretch, so take your time as you move toward Placeway Picnic Area to the north.

After leaving the picnic area, you will cross the Huron River via a road bridge, then climb to a ridge above the river. The trail continues north until intersecting the railroad tracks, then shadows the rail line for about 0.8 mile. It bends away from the tracks for about 0.7 mile, courses through a meadow, then returns to the tracks for the final eastward run toward the trailhead. Just yards from the end of the long loop, hikers cross a cement bridge, then head in to the trailhead.

Key points:

The Huron River is the centerpiece of this trail system.

Nature
Hikes

Upper Peninsula
Nature Hikes

Black bears are found in all areas of the Upper Peninsula; hikers need to be aware that Michigan's "black ghost" is always around and take precautions not to attract them to a campsite.

41 Lake Gogebic State Park

Highlights: This nature trail provides a brief glimpse of the tangled beauty of this remote corner of the Upper Peninsula and the splendor of the region's largest inland lake, and the park's namesake, Lake Gogebic.

Type of hike: Loop trail.

Total distance: 3 miles.

Difficulty: Easy to moderate.

Best months: July through October.

Map: Lake Gogebic State Park brochure and map.

Permits and fees: Modern campsites, $14 per day. State park daily vehicle pass, $4.00; annual pass, $20.00.

Special considerations: The park is open year-round, but most facilities are not available after October.

For more information: Lake Gogebic State Park, HC1 139, Marenisco, MI 49947; (906) 842-3341.

Parking and trailhead facilities: There is plenty of parking available at the picnic area; parking in the camping area is reserved for campers.

Finding the trailhead: Lake Gogebic State Park is 10 miles north of the intersection of U.S. Highway 2 and Michigan Highway 64, or 8 miles south of the intersection of Michigan Highway 28 and M-64. The park is 17 miles north of the Michigan–Wisconsin border.

The trailhead is in the day-use area at the north end of the campground. From the park entrance, turn left into the campground and drive north to the day-use area. The trailhead is in the northwest corner.

The hike:

This nature trail through the backcountry of Lake Gogebic State Park provides a brief glimpse into the tangled beauty of the western Upper Peninsula. The park is located on the western shores of the region's largest inland lake, providing a full weekend of possibilities. The park is open year-round, and the trail is accessible anytime snow is off the ground; some park facilities are closed from late October until May.

The 3-mile nature loop starts at one end of the day-use area and returns to "civilization" at the south end of the park. It is the only developed pathway in the state park and, in winter, transforms into a cross-country ski trail. The trail is easy to follow and presents no noteworthy challenges to even the casual hiker. Finding your way back through the day-use area and campground to your car might be the toughest part of the entire trek.

You can hike the trail from either end, but most hikers leave from the day-use area at the north end of the campground and return to the south end of the park. From the trailhead, hikers cross M–64, then Gillis Creek, climbing the only hill along the trail system and quickly dropping back to the level of much of the rest of the trail. The trail goes about 0.5 mile before swinging south for approximately 1 mile then turning back toward the park.

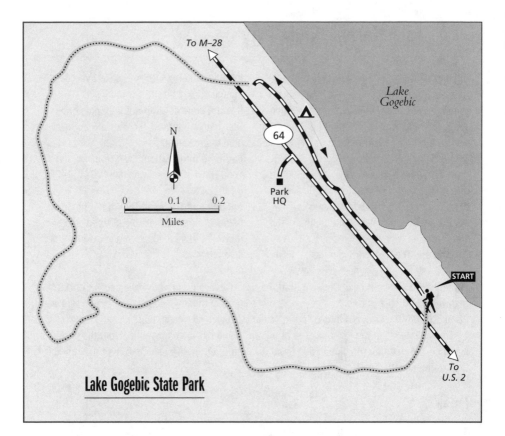

Lake Gogebic State Park

The final mile is an eastward hike through thick forest, where hikers will encounter several areas that remain soggy for days after a heavy rain. About 0.2 mile from the end of the hike, the trail swings back north, crossing M–64 for the last time, then going over a small, unnamed creek before ending in the parking lot at the southern end of the park.

Key points:

The nature trail is an easy hike and is well marked.

42 Days River Pathway

Highlights: Family-friendly and easy-to-navigate loops that can be handled by hikers of all ages and experience levels. Wildlife, fishing in the Days River, and scenery unmatched anywhere else in the region.

Type of hike: Loop hike.

Total distance: 20.7 miles.

Difficulty: Easy to moderate.

Best months: July through October.

Maps: USGS Perkins: Department of Natural Resources Days River Pathway map.

Permits and fees: None.

Special considerations: The area is a haven for hunters in the fall, so if you visit after mid-September, wear brightly colored clothing.

For more information: District Forest manager, Escanaba River State Forest, 6833 U.S. Highway 41, Gladstone, MI 49837; (906) 786-2351; Department of Natural Resources, Forest Management Office, Marquette, MI 49855; (906) 228-6561.

Parking and trailhead facilities: Parking is available at the trailhead, but services are lacking.

Finding the trailhead: The area is 3 miles north of Gladstone and the same distance south of Rapid River along U.S. Highway 2. To reach the parking area from the east, drive west from Rapid River on U.S. 2 for 3 miles, then turn right onto Days River Road. The entrance to the parking area is 0.5 mile west of the golf course. From the west, drive east on U.S. 2 from Gladstone for 3 miles to the turn onto Days River Road. The trailhead is on the south side of the parking lot.

The hike:

The Days River Pathway is a nearly 9-mile loop course through typical Upper Peninsula ecosystems, including wet river lowlands and heavily forested uplands. Hikes along the longest loop or any of the smaller loops in the area can be handled by casual hikers yet are challenging enough to hold the attention of more experienced hikers. The area offers quiet serenity, accessible from major highways. It is probably one of the best places in northern Michigan for a family hike.

The area is simply a "walk through a forest," to quote a state forest official in Gladstone. The only history along these loops is natural history, provided by the changing terrain and varying ecosystems found along the trail. White-tailed deer and other animals can be found here, along with a large number of songbirds that are seen frequently along the pathway. For those adventurous enough to make a cross-country trek, the nearby Days River offers brook trout and other aquatic life. In fall the area is ablaze in color, presenting photographers with plenty of opportunities to fill frame after frame.

The pathway's loop trails shadow the river (on northbound legs) and meander atop hardwood ridges that look down on the river (on the return trip). The trails are sandy but easy to follow. Wandering off trail to get to the river could present some challenges and is not recommended for novice hikers. Footbridges provide access across creeks, streams, and the one gorge along the trail.

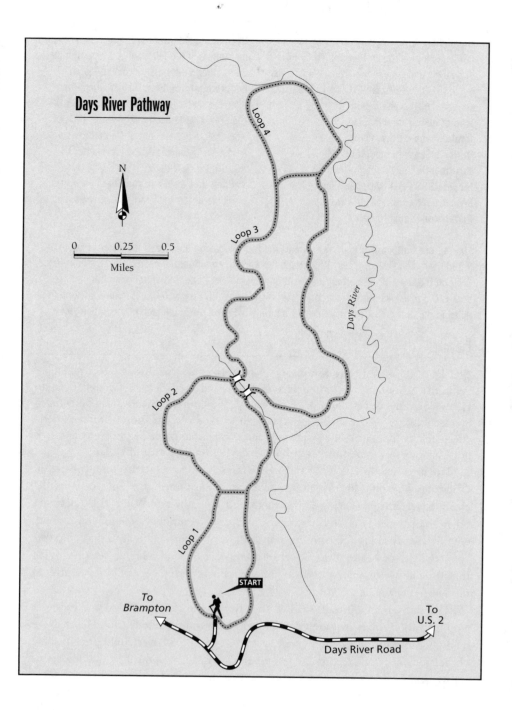

Days River Pathway

N

0   0.25   0.5
Miles

Loop 4

Loop 3

Days River

Loop 2

Loop 1

START

To
Brampton

To
U.S. 2

Days River Road

Fall is the best season to visit the area, since summer's squadrons of flying insects are gone; but deer and small-game hunters are also attracted to the trails, so dress accordingly.

The first loop, a **1.9-mile trail,** provides only a brief glimpse of the entire system but greets hikers with a footbridge over a deep river gorge at the very start of the loop. Once across the bridge, the trail heads north for 0.9 mile to a junction with the second loop and a crossover trail that will return hikers to the trailhead. This leg of the trail meanders about 300 yards back from the Days River, but the waterway is visible at points along the way. At the crossover point the connector trail heads west for just under 0.2 mile to the returning southern leg of this loop. (A cross-country ski trail crosses through the connector trail about midway across; it shouldn't present any confusion, but be aware that it is there.) The 0.8-mile trek back to the trailhead is through a forested area; approximately 0.3 mile after it turns south, the ski trail crosses the main pathway once again. Continue south and you will be fine.

To continue along the second loop, extending the hike to a **3.8-mile** jaunt, continue north from the crossover trail junction. The loop's nearest approach to the river comes as the trail passes under a major power line, bringing hikers within yards of the Days River. From this point, the trail swings northwest and 0.3 mile farther on meets the junction with the third loop. A bridge over a small creek marks the turn to start the third loop, but by staying on the creek's southern bank you can continue around the second loop to return to the trailhead. Less than 100 yards from the first bridge, a second one, the junction with the return leg of the outer loops, will appear to the right of the pathway. Keep bearing left for the return trip. About 0.6 mile down the trail, hikers will again pass under the power line, just where the ski trail again crosses the pathway. It is now less than 0.25 mile to the junction with the first loop and the final return leg.

The **6.2-mile loop** continues outward at the first footbridge over the creek. The first portion of this loop goes very near the banks of the river. The trail swings southeast of the river immediately after crossing the bridge. The next 1.4 miles to the crossover trail (used to return to the trailhead) more or less traces the course of the river but never really gets close enough to allow hikers to easily reach the water. The 0.25-mile connector swings west for the return trip to the parking lot. The final 0.8 mile of the third loop ends at the second footbridge mentioned earlier. Once across, hikers will trace the westerly edges of the first two loops to make their way back to the start point.

The fourth **8.8-mile loop** adds a 2.6-mile extension and is the outer limits of the Days River Pathway. As the trail continues north, it will come very close to the river 0.6 mile from the start of the loop and continue nearby for 0.5 mile. Once the trail bends away from the river it signals the start of the return trip to the trailhead.

Key points:

2.2 Pair of bridges linking the two outer loops with the inner loops

Lower Peninsula
Nature Hikes

43 Herman Vogler Conservation Area

Highlights: A 270-acre living outdoor class-room that includes a mix of upland and low-land habitats; a 9-acre impoundment attracts a variety of waterfowl, mainly in the fall.
Type of hike: Loop hike.
Total distance: 8 miles.
Difficulty: Moderate.
Best months: Late summer and fall.
Map: The Presque Isle County Conservation District produces a good map and brochure of the trail system and conservation area, available by writing to PICC, 240 West Erie Street, Rogers City, MI 49779. Trails are well marked

with locator map boards at critical junctions.
Permits and fees: None.
Special considerations: The area is a haven for hunters in the fall; if you visit after mid-September, wear brightly colored clothing.
For more information: Rogers City Chamber of Commerce, 292 South Bradley Highway, Rogers City, MI 49779, (989) 734-2535; Presque Isle Conservation District, 240 West Erie Street, Rogers City, MI 49779; (989) 734-4000.
Parking and trailhead facilities: Two parking areas provide more than adequate parking.

Finding the trailhead: The area is 0.5 mile north of Rogers City, just off U.S. Highway 23. Turn left onto Forest Avenue to the entrance and the parking lot. A gravel road leads to an inner parking area. The trailhead is at the east end of the outer parking lot.

The hike:

The Herman Vogler Conservation Area is a constantly changing blend of habitats that range from highland hardwoods to marshes and a nine-acre impoundment that attracts a variety of waterfowl and wildlife. The area was purchased by the State of Michigan in 1986 through the Michigan Land Trust Fund and was turned over to the Presque Isle County Soil Conservation District to be managed as a conservation education/recreation area.

The multiuse area is a 270-acre tract of public land, one-third of which lies within the city limits of Rogers City. The Trout River crosses the property for 3,500 feet, fed by a variety of smaller creeks-including the important brook trout nursery, Hartwick Creek. Forests of the area include ancient stands of cedars, mature hard-woods, and examples of forest management techniques that will ensure that the area continues to flourish. The large parcel holds more than 7 miles of trails, used by hik-ers and cross-country skiers. Hunters enjoy outstanding upland bird, snowshoe hare, and deer hunting.

Hikers have a choice right from the start, since the trailhead for all the loops is the same. The northeast loop, a 0.75-mile, easy trail moves away from the parking lot along Trout River and back toward U.S. 23. The terrain along this loop is generally flat, but the trail is a bit sandy in places, which can make travel tough. The loop trav-erses a mix of habitats including cedar swamp and upland hardwoods. This area has

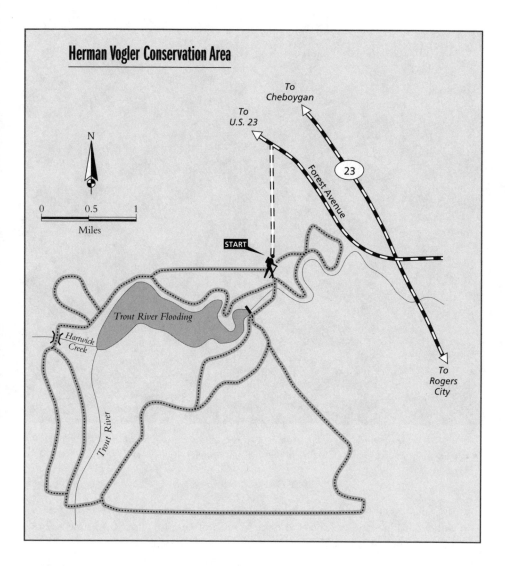

Herman Vogler Conservation Area

To
Cheboygan

To
U.S. 23

N

0   0.5   1
Miles

23

Forest Avenue

START

Trout River Flooding

Hartwick
Creek

Trout River

To
Rogers
City

been left unmanaged in its "natural" state to illustrate the tangles nature leaves behind.

Leaving the parking lot trailhead in the opposite direction, hikers will travel only a short distance along the northern shore of the Trout River impoundment before climbing up a sandy hill to the crest of a hardwood ridge that parallels the northern edge of the impoundment. The first evidence of forest management can be seen here; the area has been both clear-cut and select cut to improve stands of hardwoods and pine. At the end of the ridge, hikers drop into a wet area filled with large cedar trees and a few pockets of mature aspen and cross Hartwick Creek via a rustic wooden footbridge. This area is popular with upland bird hunters and rabbit hunters

The 270-acre Herman Vogler Conservation Area is a constantly changing blend of habitats, ranging from upland hardwood ridges to marshes and a nine-acre flooding.

in late fall. Several small creeks and wet areas are traversed along the trail by means of wooden bridges and walkways, and the route continues for about 0.75 mile before rising to hardwood ridges along the south edge of the area.

After crossing Trout River at the back edge of the property, hikers once again have a choice of trails. The left fork trail parallels the wetland area along the impoundment; the right fork winds through hardwood stands, wildlife openings, and grouse walks. Both forks join at a point overlooking the dam that created the impoundment, meandering for about 100 yards to a bridge crossing Trout River and leading back to the trailhead and the parking lot.

Key points:

The area offers plenty of challenge for hikers but is tame enough for the entire family to enjoy.

44 Grass River Natural Area

Highlights: A 1,143-acre park housing a blend of wetlands and wildlife habitat laced together by a series of trails providing enjoyable walks, bird-watching, and the chance to be lost in carpets of spring wildflowers.
Type of hike: Loop hike.
Total distance: 5.75 miles.
Difficulty: Easy.
Best months: July through October.
Maps: Grass River Natural Area trail guide; available by writing GRNA, P.O. Box 231,

Bellaire, MI 49615.
Permits and fees: None.
Special considerations: The nonprofit Grass River Natural Area Association maintains the area; memberships are available. The Tamarack Trail is wheelchair accessible.
For more information: Grass River Natural Area, P.O. Box 231, Bellaire, MI 49615; (231) 533-8314.
Parking and trailhead facilities: Parking is available at the trailhead.

Finding the trailhead: The entrance to the area is west of Mancelona off County Road 618, east of Crystal Springs. Drive west of Mancelona on CR 618 for 8.5 miles to the entrance to the Grass River Natural Area. Turn north (right) onto a dirt road for the 0.75-mile drive to the trailhead. From Crystal Springs, drive east CR 618 for 1.5 miles, then left (north) onto the dirt access road to the trailhead.

The hikes:

The Grass River Natural Area comprises a mix of habitats: upland forests, fields, creeks, rivers, marshes, and swamps. Naturalists have identified more than 60 species of fish, reptiles, and amphibians here, as well as 400 different species of plants. The area encompasses the Grass River, which is a short connecting waterway joining Clam Lake and Lake Bellaire, both part of the Chain of Lakes in Antrim County. The natural area offers a close-up view of wetland flora and fauna as well as other habitats.

Six short trails let hikers step into the area. The shortest, the Cabin Trail, is less than 0.2 mile long; the Woodland/Wildlife Trail, the longest, is 2.25 miles long. All six trails are easy hiking, requiring no special footwear or precautions. One of the trails is covered with cedar chips to make walking easy.

The **Cabin Trail** must be walked by all visitors, since it leads from the parking area to the interpretive building. Hikers will pass through a long-abandoned field and an old-growth stand of upland hardwoods before reaching the interpretive center and the start point for the other loops. The most prevalent trees in this first portion of the natural area are aspen and maple, but balsam fir, white pine, and black cherry are also present. A balsam thicket acts as a transition zone between the upland region and the wetlands.

The **Sedge Meadow Trail** starts behind the interpretive building and leads through a variety of wetland habitats, providing access to the Grass River off a short

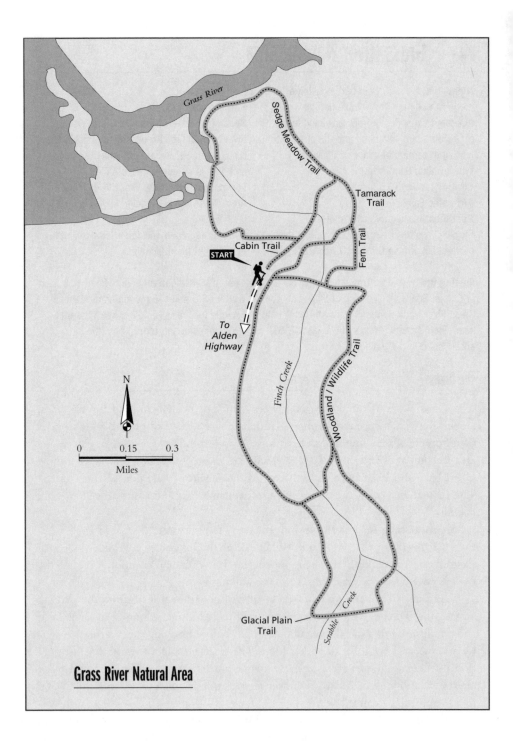

Grass River

Sedge Meadow Trail

Tamarack
Trail

Fern Trail

Cabin Trail

START

To
Alden
Highway

Finch Creek

Woodland / Wildlife Trail

N

0   0.15   0.3
Miles

Glacial Plain
Trail

Scrabble Creek

Grass River Natural Area

The upland forests of the Grass River area are filled with gourmet treats for the hiker with an eye for small tidbits like this morel mushroom.

spur trail. The main trail passes through a mix of habitats, including a cedar swamp and the sedge meadow along the river that gives it its name. The trail crosses Finch Creek; near the crossing point, it's not uncommon to catch sight of feeding or cruising brook, brown, and rainbow trout. The insect life from the swampy area provides a moving smorgasbord for the fish in the clear, cold water of the creek. Wildlife along this trail include the occasional white-tailed deer, various small furbearers, ducks, and geese.

The Sedge Meadow Trail continues to the Grass River before swinging back to join the **Tamarack Trail.** This short trail is wide and barrier-free, great for those in wheelchairs. This brief loop into the Grass River Natural Area passes through mainly wetland areas and related flora and fauna. The trail winds its way back to the interpretive center where the next trail, the Fern Trail, begins.

The 0.4-mile **Fern Trail** offers a way back to the parking lot, but the main attraction of this brief trail is that it parallels Finch Creek, offering a look into the life along the waterway.

The **Woodland/Wildlife Trail,** one of the longer trail loops in the area, shadows both flanks of Finch Creek, upland hardwoods, and swampy areas as it passes through mixed terrain. The wildlife and plant varieties match the changing habitats. Included on this route is a small pond that is a viewing area for amphibian life.

The final trail loop, the **Glacial Plain Trail,** is a 2-mile hike that affords hikers the chance to walk their own way: The marked trail ends in an open field that faces terraced hills and upland forest types. After some exploration, return to the last marked sections of the trail and hike the remainder of the Glacial Plain Trail back to the parking lot.

Key points:

Since much of the area encompasses wetlands, be prepared for soggy travel.

45 Pintail Pond Nature Trail

Highlights: A self-guided nature trail that is part of the Rifle River Recreation Area.
Type of hike: Loop hike.
Total distance: 1.5 miles.
Difficulty: Easy.
Best months: July through October.
Map: Department of Natural Resources map and brochure, available at the park entrance.
Permits and fees: Modern campsites, $15.00 per day; rustic campsites, $9.00 per day. State park daily vehicle pass, $4.00; annual pass, $20.00. (The trail system is part of adjacent Rifle River Recreation Area, and facilities are actually part of the larger area.)

Special considerations: Although this hike is rated as easy, hikers should be sure to wear comfortable shoes.
For more information: Rifle River Recreation Area, 2550 East Rose City Road, Lupton, MI 48635; (989) 473-22578.
Parking and trailhead facilities: Parking is available at the trailhead or nearby day-use areas of the Rifle River Recreation Area.

(See map on page 154.)

Finding the trailhead: Pintail Pond is located west of the entrance to the Rifle River Recreation Area. The area is 0.75 mile south of Lupton and 4.75 miles east of Rose City, off County Road F-28. From the entrance to the recreation area, turn right onto Ranch Road. The trailhead for the Pintail Pond Nature Area is across from the campground, approximately 0.5 mile.

The hike:

Pintail Pond offers a self-guided nature trail looping around watery lowlands and nearby Gamble Creek. The trail is a part of the 13-mile trail system known as the Rifle River Recreation Area (see Hike 38).

The trail is an easy hike even for the casual hiker, passing through mixed habitat approximately 1 mile north of the Rifle River. Terrain is generally flat, presenting no obstacles to hikers regardless of experience—just be sure to wear comfortable shoes.

Hikers will pass by nearly two dozen signposts pointing to a variety of environments. Those who are equipped with the brochure provided at the entrance to Pintail Pond will head west (left), entering the first of the mixed stands of hardwoods and softwoods found in the region. The floor of these stands (predominantly white birch) is covered with bracken and flowering ferns, laced together by mats of tag alder. This is the high shoulder of the area.

Large white pines make their appearance as hikers move along the west side of the nature trail. Many of these trees were overlooked by loggers at the turn of the century and have since grown to impressive sizes. Next, the clear, cool waters of Gamble Creek come into view. This premier trout stream is open during fishing season, offering good opportunities for brown trout. Lowlands indicate that hikers are nearing the shores of Pintail Pond. Cedar lowlands are common here, particularly white cedar.

Trout fishing in Gamble Creek is an outstanding diversion for hikers, particularly for brown trout anglers.

Rising out of the lowlands area, the trail soon is flanked by stands of aspen. It is not uncommon to see deer and upland birds in this area; the aspens are prime browse for big game and provide cover and food for grouse and woodcock. Hikers should stay on the established trail, since areas of vegetation are simply floating above hidden pockets of water. As the pond becomes more choked by vegetation, these areas are more prevalent and pose a danger to hikers who wander off trail. Step carefully.

The lowland bog offers a compressed look at a wide variety of plants and flowers, including mosses, sundew, yellow pond lilies, and pitcher plants. This is a great opportunity to photograph plants and birds attracted to the mix of habitats.

The short hike back to the start point is through a stand of tamarack and black spruce, matching the climb out of the wetland area. Remember to take only pictures and keep footprints on the trail to avoid damaging the area's fragile wetlands.

Key points:

Nearly two dozen signposts guide hikers around the pond.

46 Old Nursery Trail

Highlights: A walk into the history of the Civilian Conservation Corps in Michigan from the old state nursery on the north shore of Higgins Lake.
Type of hike: Loop hike.
Total distance: 1.5 miles.
Difficulty: Easy.
Best months: July through October.
Map: A brochure and map are available at the visitor center.

Permits and fees: None.
Special considerations: An easy hike that requires only time to enjoy.
For more information: Park Supervisor, North Higgins Lake State Park, 11511 West Higgins Lake Drive, Roscommon, MI 48653; (989) 821–6125; Roscommon Chamber of Commerce, Roscommon, MI 48653.
Parking and trailhead facilities: Parking is available at the trailhead.

Finding the trailhead: The park is about 10 miles west of Roscommon, on the north shore of Higgins Lake. From the north the loop is about 10 miles south of Grayling off Old U.S. Highway 27. The trailhead is adjacent to Park Headquarters. From Roscommon take County Road 203 west for 10 miles to the headquarters building. From U.S. 27 take the Roscommon exit east for 1 mile to the headquarters entrance.

The hike:

The self-guided Old Nursery Nature Trail is a 1.5-mile loop through the remains of a 700-bed tree nursery area that supplied state and private planting efforts in the early 1900s.

The largest appeal of this quiet area is the forest, but the rich history preserved here receives the most attention. On the south side of CR 203, just east of the trailhead, is the Ralph MacMullan Center, built by Civilian Conservation Corps (CCC) troops in the 1920s. This CCC museum site contains historic buildings, a fire tower, and other displays.

The Old Nursery Trail is a brief visit through various stations in the old state nursery. The twenty-three signposts along this self-guided trail make this an enjoyable 1.5-mile loop. The trail can be hiked clockwise or counterclockwise; the trail description given here follows the signposts to avoid confusion. Starting at the trailhead: Signpost 1 indicates the newly constructed and recreated Civilian Conservation Corps Museum.

Signposts 2 and 3 detail the area once covered by the 700-bed seed nursery used to start seedlings exported from the facility and more of the nursery grounds.

Signpost 4 notes the remains of the irrigation and sprinkler system used to water the seedlings and seedbeds.

Signpost 5 marks the site of the nursery's icehouse, circa 1912. Signpost 6 shows the packing house where seedlings were bundled for shipment.

Signpost 7 indicates a 1913 model fire tower.

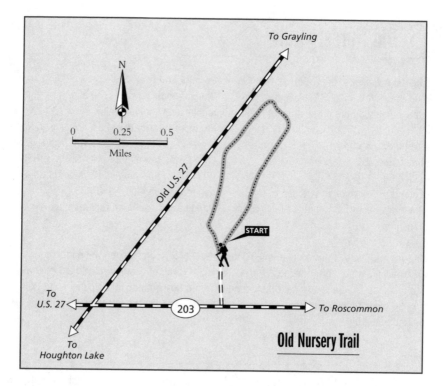

Signposts then move into the forest. Signpost 8 is in a mature forest area, which was the actual boundary of the nursery. Signpost 9 comes with plots of red pine. The trees here were originally scheduled to be transplanted, but were not actually transplanted. Signpost 10 shows a thinned stand used to exemplify this style of preproduction grooming. Signpost 11 marks a comparison stand, not thinned at all, to show the effects of no management in a red pine stand.

The signs also indicate natural features. Signpost 12 highlights sweet ferns, common along the trail. Signpost 13 shows an area that was burned over at the turn of the century. Signpost 14 offers a view from the top of the rim above Higgins Lake, some 126 feet above the lake's surface.

Signpost 15 comes in a new growth area that has sprouted as the result of a commercial clearcut.

Signpost 16 indicates maple-leaf viburnum.

Signpost 17 shows hikers an example of a "nurse log," where remains of a decaying log feed forest growth. Signpost 18 gives another example of the natural selection process in the forest.

The steel fire tower that once stood at the site of Signpost 19 is the same one that has been reconstructed in the CCC Museum area near the trailhead.

Old Nursery Trail is alive with splashes of bright color from berries and wildflowers.

Near this site of Signpost 20 are the remains of the 105,000-gallon concrete cistern that supplied water for the irrigation system for the nursery.

Signpost 21 is a "take a break" point that encourages visitors to listen for the sounds of the forest.

Signpost 22 describes jack pine, one of this area's most common species. Signpost 23 points to the black locust, an important food source for small animals.

After you've passed all the above signs, you've made the loop. Your next stop is the CCC Museum and the trailhead.

Key points:

Twenty-three signposts guide hikers around this 1.5-mile loop trail.

47 Tobico Marsh Trail

Highlights: The Tobico Marsh trail system provides a chance to explore a mix of wetland habitats that are home to more than 200 species of birds and a glimpse of rare flora and fauna usually found only in larger, more remote wetlands in northern Michigan.

Type of hike: Loop hike.

Total distance: 4 miles.

Difficulty: Easy.

Best months: July through October.

Maps: USGS Kawkawlin; Tobico Marsh State Game Area map, provided at nature center.

Permits and fees: Modern campsites, with fees ranging from $13 to $15 per night depending on hookups available. State park daily vehicle pass, $4.00; annual pass, $20.00.

Special considerations: Interpretive and school programs are available by arrangement.

For more information: Department of Natural Resources, Bay City State Park, 3582 State Park Drive, Bay City, MI 48706; (989) 684-3020. Or call the DNR District Wildlife Biologist in Clare, Michigan, at (989) 386-7991.

Parking and trailhead facilities: Parking is available at the trailhead.

Finding the trailhead: The area is about 5 miles east of Interstate 75, and 5 miles north of Bay City. The entrance to the marsh is 0.5 mile north of Bay City State Park.

From I-75 take exit 168 and head east on Beaver Road. The entrance to Bay City State Park and the Nature Center is 5 miles from the exit on Killarney Road, just past the junction of Beaver Road and Michigan Highway 247. The trailhead is 0.5 mile north of the Nature Center.

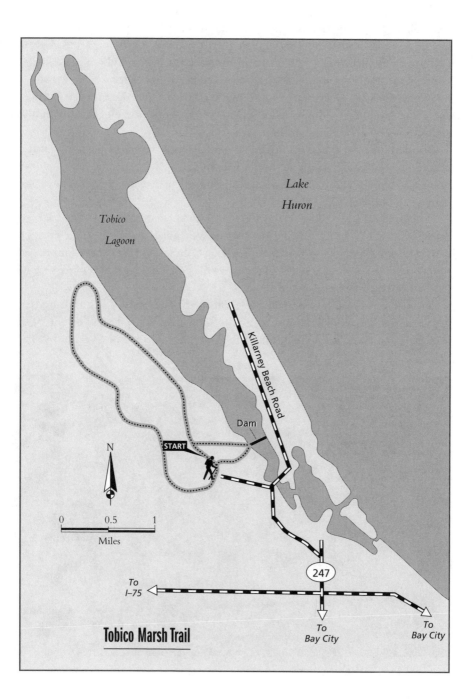

Lake
Huron

Tobico
Lagoon

Killarney Beach Road

Dam

START

N

0   0.5   1
Miles

247

To
I–75

To
Bay City

To
Bay City

Tobico Marsh Trail

The hike:

The Tobico Marsh wetland habitats are home to varied wildlife and more than 200 species of birds. DNR biologists estimate that as many as 6,000 ducks and geese filter through the marsh as they migrate south in the fall. The area also offers a glimpse of rare Michigan flora and fauna that's only duplicated in larger, remote marshes in northern Michigan. Deer, beaver, mink, muskrat, more than a dozen species of ducks and geese, more than 100 species of songbirds and shorebirds, plus rare wildflowers and shrubs can all be found in the area.

Located nearly within Bay City, the area is adjacent to some of the finest offshore waterfowl hunting opportunities in the state of Michigan. Once the private possession of a hunting club that never boasted more than ten members, the area now belongs to the people of the state.

The centerpiece of the area, the 900-acre Tobico Lagoon, provides the backdrop for this nature hike and is the magnet that draws animals and birds to the area. The 4-mile walking loop along the lagoon's western shore lets hikers peer into the life of the marsh. It's an easy hike for all members of the family, regardless of experience. Good footwear is recommended.

From the trailhead, hikers will go less than 0.5 mile to a short loop trail and detour that leads to a dike; this side jaunt affords hikers a great view of one of the lagoon's cattail marshes at the southern end of Tobico Lagoon and is an excellent

The 900-acre Tobico Lagoon is the centerpiece of this nature area, and the creatures that inhabit it are often more than willing to pose for a quick picture.

viewing and photo site for numerous species of birds. The hike out to the dike is not a loop, so you will need to retrace your steps to return to the main pathway. Before reaching the main trail, you will pass the first of the observation towers in the marsh.

There is nothing complicated about the hike on the main trail—it's simply a scenic walk around Tobico Marsh. Nearly 1 mile from the junction with the short spur to the dike, hikers will reach the Tobico Marsh Interpretive Area. The area is a great spot for a break; it features a second observation tower and a boardwalk offering a look into the center of the lagoon.

From the "break area," it's nearly 1.5 miles around the back side of the refuge. Hikers will have plenty of opportunity to view birdlife. According to state waterfowl biologists, the marsh is a major stopover for ducks and geese migrating along the Lake Huron shoreline. Hikers enter a wooded area just about 1 mile before they complete the loop and reach the trailhead. For many hikers, this is just enough time to decide whether to make a second circuit, another trip to the dike, or plan a return visit when waterfowl viewing is at its peak.

Key points:

The interpretive trail is well marked and easy to follow for hikers of all experience levels.

48 Sleeper State Park

Highlights: Nearly 1,000 acres of forest, wetlands, and sandy beach and dunes along Saginaw Bay of Lake Huron. The 4 miles of marked trails are the only designated pathways in the park, but adventurous hikers can explore anywhere they can walk.

Type of hike: Loop hike.

Total distance: 4.8 miles.

Difficulty: Easy.

Best months: July through September.

Maps: USGS Rush Lake; Department of Natural Resources Albert E. Sleeper State Park

map and self-guided trail brochures.

Permits and fees: Modern campsites are available for $18 per night depending on hookups available. State park daily vehicle pass, $4.00; annual pass, $20.00.

Special considerations: Good footwear is a must; sandy trails can be difficult to hike.

For more information: Albert E. Sleeper State Park, Caseville, MI 48725; (989) 856–4411.

Parking and trailhead facilities: Parking is available in the day-use area, but hikers cannot use the camping area for overflow parking.

Finding the trailhead: The park is reached from the west by driving 5 miles east from Caseville on Michigan Highway 25. The day-use area is on the left; the campground and trail system are on the right. Hikers coming in from the east can reach the park by driving 12 miles west from Port Austin on M–25.

Each of the four trails is accessible from both the campground and the outdoor center, but the campground trailhead is the easier to access. From M–25 turn south into the campground. The trailhead is located between sites 66 and 68.

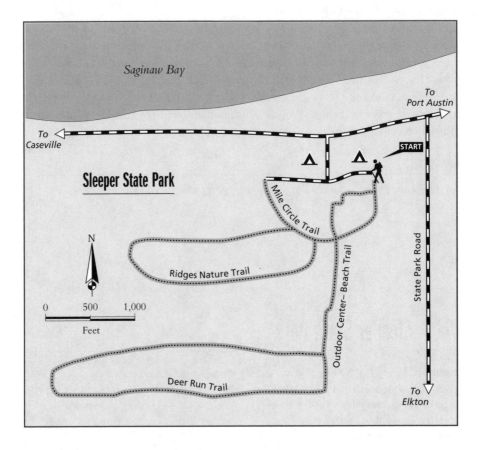

The hikes:

This heavily forested state park offers the best of all situations for a vacationing hiker, with nearly 1,000 acres of forest to explore and the beauty and expanse of the Lake Huron shoreline just a short walk out of the trees. The park is divided by M–25, with the day-use area and beaches to the north and the campground and nature trails to the south of the highway. The area's 280 campsites attract plenty of use during the summer, but the heavy pine forest separates the activity in the campground from the

The Lake Huron shoreline is a popular destination for migrating waterfowl and shorebirds each spring and fall.

serenity of the woods. Set back in the park is an outdoor center off State Park Road, offering an opportunity for large groups of nature lovers to avoid crowded areas nearer the highway.

The park's hiking trails go through mature forest, over sand dunes, and through open areas with a mix of grasses and shrubs. The trails are generally empty and offer a great opportunity to view and photograph a mix of ecosystems and species, since the terrain attracts a great many birds and wild creatures, including white-tailed deer.

The area's one linear trail, the **Outdoor Center–Beach Trail,** is a 0.3-mile pathway that, as its name implies, connects the Outdoor Center with the rest of the park and, more important to some, the half-mile of beach on the north side of M–25. This trail also provides access to the 2-mile loop known as **Deer Run Trail,** which makes the deepest intrusion into the interior of the park.

From the campground south of M–25, the trail between campsites 66 and 68 provides access to the **Mile Circle Trail,** offering a brief look into the nature of the park without requiring a major commitment. The final trail, the 1.5-mile **Ridges Nature Trail,** is a brochure-equipped self-guided nature trail reached by hiking south along the Mile Circle Trail for 300 yards. The loop passes through the diverse ecosystems that make up Sleeper State Park. After completing the nature trail, hikers can either backtrack along the Mile Circle Trail, continue the transit, or detour south at the junction with the linear trail and take in the Deer Run Trail. The point of decision is a junction less than 200 feet from the end of the nature trail.

Key points:

The trail loops are on the south side of M-25 and are easy to follow.

49 Price Nature Center

Highlights: A mix of habitats attracts birds and wildlife in a gentle trail system; 200-years-old beeches and maples.
Type of hike: Loop hike.
Total distance: 2.7 miles.
Difficulty: Easy.
Best months: July through September.
Map: Price Nature Center trail map brochure.
Permits and fees: None.
Special considerations: All three trails share the same trailhead but meander through different habitats.

For more information: Price Nature Center, Saginaw County Parks and Recreation Commission, 111 South Michigan Avenue, Saginaw, MI 48602.
Parking and trailhead facilities: There is adequate parking at the trailhead west of Sheridan Road. There are no amenities at the trailhead, but camping is available at the north end of the nature center. Benches and rustic rest shelters are available along the hike route.

Finding the trailhead: The trailhead is 6 miles south of Saginaw on Sheridan Road.

The hikes:

The three trail loops in the Price Nature Center will appeal to many hikers. The mix of habitat attracts birds and wildlife, and the gentle nature of the trails makes this area an easy one-day outing. All three trails share the same start point but traverse different habitats.

The first, the **White Oak Trail,** is a 1-mile loop with a connector trail that can be used to cut about 0.2 mile off the hike if you decide to head back early. From the trailhead the hike begins to the right. Hikers will find the going easy as they

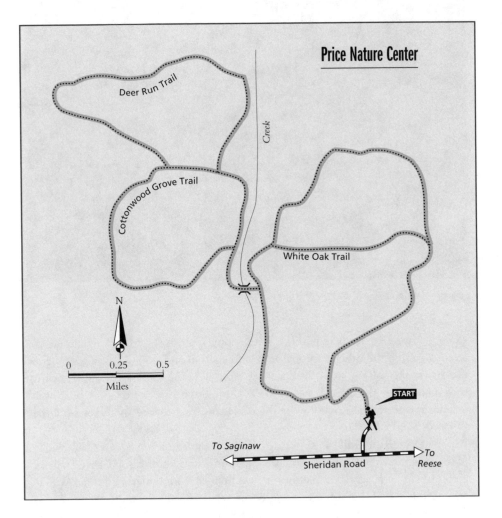

Deer Run Trail

Creek

Cottonwood Grove Trail

White Oak Trail

N

| 0 | 0.25 | 0.5 |

Miles

START

To Saginaw

Sheridan Road

To Reese

enter the newest part of the forest, filled mostly with birch and aspen. After a few hundred yards the forest changes and hikers enter a mature stand of maple and beech that has been untouched for nearly 200 years. A signpost on the left marks the turn for the connector trail; the main trail continues to a trail shelter located at about the halfway point in the loop.

The connector trail reenters the loop about 0.25 mile from the shelter as you pass through more forest. The start of the Cottonwood Grove Trail loop is less than 100 yards from this junction. The junction gives you two options: Head back the remaining 0.25 mile to the trailhead, or make the right turn, cross a small footbridge over a small creek, and start on the **Cottonwood Grove Trail.**

This trail loop shadows the creek for several hundred yards before turning into the forest. Its first junction with the Deer Run Trail offers hikers the option of

Fungi adorn a dead tree at Price Nature Center.

extending the hike to include this 0.7-mile loop. Cottonwood Grove continues on around, passing the other end of the Deer Run Trail and stopping at a trail shelter that marks the halfway point of this loop. From here the trail moves onto a boardwalk because of the mucky nature of the soil along this stretch. The boardwalk extends for nearly 0.25 mile before the trail turns back toward the creek on a trail that is dry and a bit sandy.

The **Deer Run Trail** offers perhaps the best opportunity to observe the wildlife of the area. Just over 100 yards from the junction with Cottonwood Grove Trail, this loop stops at an observation platform that is popular with birders and other wildlife watchers. The trail then follows a section of railroad tracks for more than 0.3 mile. This stretch of the loop is a favorite feeding area for a variety of birds because of the berry bushes and other flowering shrubs found along the trail. From here the trail turns back left for 0.3 mile and rejoins the Cottonwood Grove Trail.

Total hiking time for all three loops is a casual two and a half hours, allowing plenty of time to observe the beauty of the Price Nature Center. *Note:* There is camping on the north end of the complex, but it is for organized groups only, available by reservation.

Key points:

Signposts direct hikers around each of the three loops in the trail system.

50 For-Mar Nature Preserve

Highlights: Nature study areas, trails, and an arboretum for developing trees, vines, and shrubs planted in the park.
Type of hike: Loop hike.
Total distance: 6.7 miles.
Difficulty: Easy.
Best months: July through October.
Maps: The Genesee County Parks and Recreation Commission supplies all visitors with an excellent map.

Permits and fees: None.
Special considerations: The park is an active education and environmental center and may be the scene of classroom sessions during spring and fall when school is in session.
For more information: For-Mar Nature Preserve, G–5360 East Potter Road, Burton, MI 48509; (810) 789-8548.
Parking and trailhead facilities: Adequate parking is available at the Education Center.

Finding the trailhead: For-Mar is within 1 mile of Flint, just west of Belsay Road. The main entrance is located on East Potter Road, and there is a pedestrian entrance along the park's western boundary, off Genesee Road. To reach the main entrance, drive east from Flint on Interstate 69 to Belsay Road, then drive north 2 miles to Potter Road and turn left onto East Potter Road. Go 0.3 mile to the entrance. The main trailhead is on the south side of the DeWaters Education Center, just inside the main entrance to the park.

The hikes:

For-Mar is Genesee County's finest example of what caring and concern can create in a highly urbanized area. The park's 380–acre wildlife preserve and arboretum were opened in 1970 by the Genesee County Parks and Recreation Commission.

The preserve is visited annually by thousands of hikers, birders, and urban residents just looking for open space. Only 1 mile from the city limits of Flint, For-Mar is an active education and environmental study center, open to everyone.

The Genesee and Michigan Audubon Clubs have joined together to sponsor the Croyden Foote Bird Collection, a must-stop for visitors. The exhibit is located in the interpretive building on the west boundary of the preserve. There is always a great deal of birdlife in the area. The ponds and floodings attract few waterfowl, but the woodlands and wetlands draw a wide variety of songbirds to the park. Hikers have plenty of opportunities to photograph the dozens of species that regularly visit the area, particularly along the trails that shadow the creek dividing the preserve nearly in two. In season, wildflowers paint a vivid backdrop.

The nearly 7 miles of trails in the nature preserve trace the shorelines of ponds and floodings as well as the banks of Kearsley Creek, offering visitors a close-up look at water-related habitats. The trails are all easy to follow and allow for plenty of side trips to all corners of the park.

From the trailhead at the DeWaters Education Center, the first loop is the **Edge**

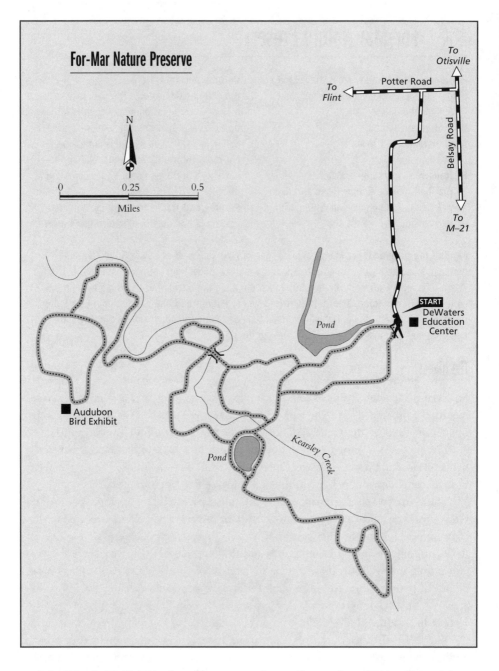

For-Mar Nature Preserve

To Otisville

Potter Road

To Flint

Belsay Road

To M–21

N

0   0.25   0.5
Miles

START
DeWaters Education Center

Pond

Audubon Bird Exhibit

Pond

Kearsley Creek

of the Woods Trail. This short loop traces the southern edge of Runoff Pond, but stops short of actually entering the wooded area along the creek. It is primarily a walking trail, not an exploring trail.

The **Sugar Bush Trail,** along the eastern banks of Kearsley Creek, joins other

The red fox finds plenty of prey animals in the preserve's nooks and crannies.

loops to create a long loop along both flanks of the waterway. Bridges provide dry foot crossings of the creek as hikers add the loops created by the **Hawthorne, Ground Water Pond, Succession, Short Loop,** and **Young Wood Trails** to extend the hike into a nearly 7-mile trek through the preserve.

From the end of the Short Loop Trail, hikers can stop and visit the Audubon Bird Exhibit near the west entrance to the preserve. A short hike south along a paved access road will bring hikers to the other must-see point in the park—the 113-acre arboretum in the preserve's southwest corner. Grass- and dirt-covered trails make walking easy, and trail markers make finding your way around For-Mar a simple task.

Key points:

0.0 DeWaters Education Center

3.5 Croyden Foote Bird Collection

3.7 Arboretum

51 Woldumar Nature Center

Highlights: The 188-acre nature center includes a large forested area, home to a variety of hardwood and wildlife species. The area also includes ponds and wetlands, focus for a large number of birds and other wildlife.

Type of hike: Loop hike.

Total distance: 5 miles.

Difficulty: Moderate.

Best months: July through October.

Map: Woldumar Nature Center map and brochure supplied at the site.

Permits and fees: None.

Special considerations: The Moon Log Cabin,

the original Anderson farm, and a number of wildlife observation platforms.

For more information: Woldumar Nature Center, 5539 Lansing Road, Lansing, MI 48917; (517) 322-0030.

Parking and trailhead facilities: Adequate parking is available at the interpretive center. Finding the trailhead: The center is 2 miles southwest of Lansing, off Lansing and Waverly Roads. The trails start at a point between the interpretive center and the barn south of the parking lot. Trails and loops spur off from other routes.

Finding the trailhead: The center is 2 miles southwest of Lansing, off Lansing and Waverly Roads. The trails start at a point between the interpretive center and the barn south of the parking lot. Trails and loops spur off from other routes.

The hikes:

Woldumar Nature Center was established in 1966 when Gladys Olds Anderson donated 177 acres from her family farm. The center has since expanded to its present 188 acres and serves as a natural sanctuary for a wide variety of wildlife amidst the urban sprawl of the state capital. Woldumar contains a variety of habitats, including fields and orchards, conifers, hardwoods, and ponds as well as 1 mile of frontage on the Grand River. It is an escape from the hustle of the city without making a long drive, and many who visit feel that they are "up north."

Deer, fox, raccoon, other animals, and dozens of bird species live in the preserve. Woldumar's habitats are all left to the whims of nature, which continuously improves the complexion of the preserve. The old farmlands have begun to revert back to natural seedings; the pine plantations of the 1940s continue to provide a quiet break for many creatures. The area's ponds, swamps, and more than a mile of river frontage all provide a perfect setting for wildlife.

Woldumar's trails are well marked and easy to follow. Hikers can take self-guided nature trails or take part in one of the many programs offered by the staff. The preserve includes three loops and three connector trails, all of which could be easily hiked in a single day. There are several steep hills, but steps assist you in getting over these obstacles. All the trails are designed to expose hikers to the many environments of the sanctuary without disturbing the natural life cycle progression of its residents.

The longest loop, the **Woods Waters Loop,** is 1.5 miles long and runs north-

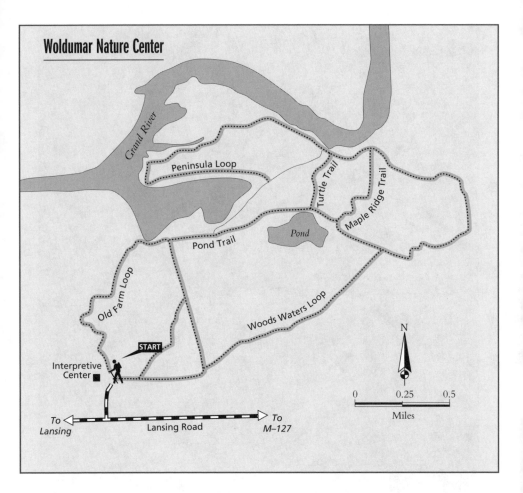

Woldumar Nature Center

Grand River

Peninsula Loop

Turtle Trail

Maple Ridge Trail

Pond Trail

Pond

Old Farm Loop

Woods Waters Loop

START

Interpretive
Center ■

N

To ◁
Lansing

Lansing Road

To
M–127

0   0.25   0.5

Miles

south through the sanctuary, touching on virtually all the different habitats. From the interpretive center, the trail heads generally south, first through a wooded area and then into an open field. The abandoned farm field is gradually being returned to a natural grassland; it's easy to see the progression that will one day develop a hardwood forest on the site.

The first junction with another trail is 0.6 mile from the trailhead. Here the long loop meets the western end of the **Pond Trail,** a 0.3-mile connector trail that bypasses much of the southern end of the sanctuary. The main pathway jogs west a bit, then finishes the southward trace around a large marshy area near the southern boundary of the sanctuary. In spring the birdlife in the marsh can be beautiful to watch and hear, but the high-pitched whine of insects can spoil the whole scene.

Once around the southern end of the marsh, the trail swings east for about 300 yards to the junction with the southern end of the **Maple Ridge Trail,** a 0.1-mile connector trail leading north to the Pond Trail. Past this junction, the pathway passes

These twin fawns are a prime example of the quality and mix of habitats found in the area.

along the bank of the Grand River and, 100 yards farther on, reaches the southern end of the **Turtle Trail,** another 0.1-mile connector trail leading north to the Pond Trail.

Just a few yards farther east, the trail swings north away from the river. At this point the main trail meets the junction with the **Peninsula Loop,** a 0.6-mile meander along one of the peninsulas jutting into the Grand River. You continue north through a wooded area for more than 100 yards, stepping out of the trees to reach the junction with the other end of the Peninsula Loop and catch a glimpse of the lagoon created by a backwater of the river. From this point you will hike in and out of the trees along the shores of the lagoon for several hundred yards. The eastern junction of the Pond Trail is passed just after you reenter the woods.

About 100 yards farther down trail, the main pathway reaches a junction with the **Old Farm Loop,** a 0.6-mile route through the remnants of the old Anderson family farm. The main trail swings west along the edge of the abandoned farm field, and the Old Farm Loop swings back north about midway along the edge of the field. The main pathway continues west to the point where the trail first exited the trees at the start of the hike.

The return trip to the trailhead is a retracing of the first few hundred yards to the interpretive center. The steepest sections of the trails and loops found in Woldumar are along the eastern edge of the Old Farm Loop, about midway along the Maple Ridge Trail. The three steep hills have steps built into their faces to assist with the climb. A few footbridges have been built to keep feet dry. The rest of the trail is wide and easy to walk. Take the time to study the map provided at the interpretive center before setting out for a day of exploring.

Key points:

0.6 Remnants of Anderson farm

4.0 Peninsula Loop along the Grand River

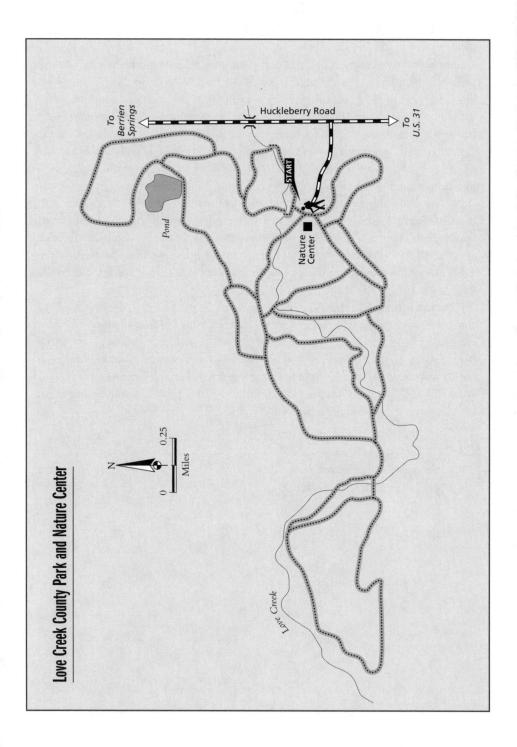

Love Creek County Park and Nature Center

52 Love Creek County Park and Nature Center

Highlights: A mix of environments, ranging from meadows and marshlands to mature forests and a pond. Birds and wildflowers arrive in spring, wildlife visits all year, and autumn colors precede winter's snow.

Type of hike: Loop hike.

Total distance: 5 miles.

Difficulty: Moderate.

Best months: Year-round.

Map: A trail map is provided at the interpretive center.

Permits and fees: None.

Special considerations: The trails are all well marked and easy to follow, but there are no shortcuts once you start. Plan your day's outing with plenty of food and water and, above all, enough time to complete the hike.

For more information: Love Creek Nature Center, 9228 Huckleberry Road, Berrien Center, MI 49102; (616) 471-2617.

Parking and trailhead facilities: Parking is located at the entrance to the park. An interpretive center, classrooms, and exhibits are at the trailhead.

Finding the trailhead: The park is located 2 miles east of the city of Berrien Springs. Take Pokagon Road southeast from Berrien Center for about 2 miles, and turn left onto Huckleberry Road. The park entrance is about 0.5 mile north.

Spring and summer, the nature center is a living classroom of nature in Michigan.

The hikes:

The hiking trails at this one-hundred-acre nature center are accessible year-round, allowing a look at complete lifecycles of this urban "wilderness."

The park is managed as a preservation and education area complete with an interpretive center, classrooms, and exhibits. There are several wooden bridges and an observation tower overlooking the park's marshy areas. Love Creek Nature Center offers 5 miles of interconnected trails that are broken down into more than a dozen loops, ranging from 0.5 to 3 miles. The possible combinations of loops can stretch a short hike into an all-day affair. Combinations of loops will take hikers through open meadows, marshland, and mature forests and along the flanks of Love Creek.

All hikes originate at the nature center, which is just 300 yards west of the entrance to the park. The trail systems course through hilly terrain and wet areas, covered by bridges and a boardwalk. Trails are sandy but provide firm footing.

The shortest loop trail, the **Marsh Trail,** is only 0.5 mile long. The trail heads southeast for nearly 0.25 mile before swinging west to shoulder the park's only marsh. About 100 yards after the turn north, hikers have the opportunity to stop and climb the 10-foot observation tower overlooking the marsh. About 200 yards past the observation tower, hikers reach the junction with the loop made up of **Trails 3** and **4,** which circles a large meadow area. Continuing north, hikers will return to the Nature Center in about 100 yards.

To the north of the nature center, **Trails 7** and **8** move through a forested area before breaking into open terrain and tracing the northern and eastern shores of a small pond. The pond attracts birds, including wood ducks and mallards, but its heavily vegetated surface does not leave room for many species.

The long loops, **Trails 10, 11,** and **12,** cover about 3 miles along the southern edge of the park, from east to west. The trails cross Love Creek a number of times, but bridges make those crossings easy and dry. The trails loop through heavy woods consisting chiefly of maple and beech. The trails are all well marked and easy to follow, but keep in mind that the loops often offer no shortcuts, especially at the extreme western edge. Plan your day's outing with sufficient food and water, not to mention time.

Key points:

Trail Loops 7 and 8, to the north of the interpretive center, circle a small pond featuring a mix of wetland environments.

Appendix A

A Hiker's Checklist

Hikers will take almost anything they choose into the woods but often forget an essential item. Day hikers should always bring maps and water and adequate clothing for the season. The list below offers a guide for hikers who intend to camp overnight or make extensive day trips in remote country. Take a final look at this checklist before you load your pack into the car.

Clothing

- ❏ Shirt
- ❏ Pants
- ❏ Underwear (extras)
- ❏ Windbreaker
- ❏ Vest
- ❏ Belt and/or suspenders
- ❏ Jacket or down parka
- ❏ Turtleneck
- ❏ Poncho or rain suit
- ❏ Gloves
- ❏ Hat
- ❏ Bandana
- ❏ Walking shorts
- ❏ Sweater
- ❏ Swimming suit
- ❏ Balaclava or headband

Shelter

- ❏ Tent
- ❏ Tent poles
- ❏ Rain/storm fly
- ❏ Tent repair kit
- ❏ Sleeping bag
- ❏ Sleeping pad

Cooking

- ❏ Matches (extras)
- ❏ Matches (waterproof)
- ❏ Waterproof match case

- ❏ Stove/fuel bottles (filled)
- ❏ Funnel
- ❏ Foam pad for stove
- ❏ Cleaning wire for stove
- ❏ Cleaning pad for stove
- ❏ Cleaning pad for pans
- ❏ Fire starter
- ❏ Cook kit
- ❏ Pot gripper
- ❏ Spatula
- ❏ Cup
- ❏ Bowl/plate
- ❏ Utensils
- ❏ Dishrag
- ❏ Dish towel
- ❏ Plastic bottle

Food and drink

- ❏ Cereal
- ❏ Bread
- ❏ Crackers
- ❏ Cheese
- ❏ Margarine
- ❏ Powdered soups
- ❏ Salt/pepper
- ❏ Main-course meals
- ❏ Snacks
- ❏ Hot chocolate
- ❏ Tea/coffee
- ❏ Powdered milk
- ❏ Drink mixes

Photography

- ❏ Camera
- ❏ Film (extra)
- ❏ Extra lenses
- ❏ Filters
- ❏ Close-up attachments
- ❏ Tripod
- ❏ Lens brush/paper
- ❏ Light meter
- ❏ Flash equipment

Fishing

- ❏ Rods
- ❏ Reels
- ❏ Flies
- ❏ Dry-fly floater (silicone)
- ❏ Lures
- ❏ Leader
- ❏ Extra line
- ❏ Swivels
- ❏ Hooks
- ❏ Split shot/sinkers
- ❏ Floats
- ❏ Bait

Miscellaneous

- ❏ Pocket or Swiss Army knife
- ❏ Whetstone
- ❏ Compass
- ❏ Topographic map
- ❏ Other maps
- ❏ Sunglasses
- ❏ Flashlight batteries (extra)
- ❏ Bulbs
- ❏ Candle lantern
- ❏ First-aid kit
- ❏ Snakebite kit
- ❏ Survival kit

- ❏ Repair kit
- ❏ Suntan lotion
- ❏ Insect repellent
- ❏ Zinc oxide (for sunburn)
- ❏ Toilet paper
- ❏ Space blanket
- ❏ Binoculars
- ❏ Nylon cord
- ❏ Plastic bags
- ❏ Rubber bands/ties
- ❏ Whistle
- ❏ Salt tablets
- ❏ Emergency fishing gear
- ❏ Wallet/I.D. cards
- ❏ Money
- ❏ Ripstop tape
- ❏ Notebook and pencils
- ❏ Field guides
- ❏ Toothpaste and toothbrush
- ❏ Dental floss
- ❏ Mirror
- ❏ Garbage bag
- ❏ Book
- ❏ Towel
- ❏ Safety pins
- ❏ Scissors
- ❏ Trowel
- ❏ Water purification tablets
- ❏ Car key
- ❏ Signal flare
- ❏ Watch
- ❏ Extra parts for stove, pack, and tent
- ❏ Solar still kit
- ❏ Rubber tubing

Appendix B

Sources for More Information

National Parks and Lakeshores

Isle Royale National Park
87 North Ripley Street
Houghton, MI 49931

Isle Royale *Queen* Ferry
Copper Harbor, MI 49918
(906) 482–4950

Isle Royale Custom Charters
(906) 337–4993

Sleeping Bear Dunes National
  Lakeshore
P.O. Box 277
9922 Front Street
Empire, MI 49630
(616) 326–5134

National Forests

Munising Ranger District
Hiawatha National Forest
601 Cedar Street
Munising, MI 49862
(906) 387–2512

Rapid River Ranger District
Hiawatha National Forest
8181 U.S. Highway 2
Rapid River, MI 49878
(906) 474–6442

District Ranger
Huron National Forest
Harrisville Ranger District
Harrisville, MI 48740
(989) 724–5431

State Forests and Parks

Michigan Department of Natural
  Resources
Forest Management Division
P.O. Box 30452
Lansing, MI 48909-7952
(517) 373–1275

Michigan Department of Natural
  Resources
Parks and Recreation Division
P.O. Box 30028
Lansing, MI 48909
(517) 373–1275

Albert E. Sleeper State Park
Caseville, MI 48725
(989) 856–4411

Bay City State Park
3582 State Park Drive
Bay City, MI 48706
(989) 684–3020

Escanaba River State Forest
6833 U.S. Highway 41/2
Gladstone, MI 49837
(906) 786–2351

Island Lake Recreation Area
12950 East Grand River
Brighton, MI 48116
(810) 229–7067

Lake Gogebic State Park
HCI 139
Marenisco, MI 49947
(906) 842–3341

Lake Superior State Forest
P.O. Box 445
Newberry, MI 49868

North Higgins State Park
11511 West Higgins Lake Drive
Roscommon, MI 48653
(989) 821–6125

Michigan Department of Natural
    Resources
Region II Headquarters
Pigeon River Country State Forest
Roscommon, MI 48653
(989) 275–5151

Michigan Department of Natural
    Resources
Stephenson, MI 49987
(906) 753–6317

Michigan Department of Natural
    Resources
P.O. Box 667
Gaylord, MI 49735
(989) 732–3541

Michigan Department of Natural
    Resources
Forest Management Regional Office
Marquette, MI 49855
(906) 228–6561

Pinckney State Recreation Area
    Headquarters
8555 Silverhill
Pinckney, MI 48169

Porcupine Mountains Wilderness
    State Park
599 Michigan Highway 107
Ontonagon, MI 49953
(906) 885–5275

Proud Lake Recreation Area
3500 Wixom Road
Milford, MI 48382
(248) 685–2433

Rifle River Recreation Area
2550 East Rose City Road
Lupton, MI 48635
(989) 473–2258

Shingleton Forest Area
Michigan Highway 28
Shingleton, MI 49884

Sylvania Wilderness Visitor Center
P.O. Box 276
Watersmeet, MI 49969
(906) 358–4724

Waterloo State Recreation Area
    Headquarters
16345 McClure Road
Chelsea, MI 48169

Watersmeet Ranger Station
Watersmeet, MI 49969
(906) 358–4551

Nature Centers and Wildlife Refuges

For-Mar Nature Preserve
G-5360 East Potter Road
Burton, MI 48509
(810) 789–8548

Grass River Natural Area
P.O. Box 231
Bellaire, MI 49615
Summer (231) 533–8576
Office (231) 533–8314

Love Creek Nature Center
9228 Huckleberry Road
Berrien Center, MI 49102
(616) 471–2617

Price Nature Center
County of Saginaw Parks and
    Recreation Commission
111 South Michigan Avenue
Saginaw, MI 48602

Seney National Wildlife Refuge
HCR #2, Box 1
Seney, MI 49883
(906) 586–9851

Woldumar Nature Center
5539 Lansing Road
Lansing, MI 48917
(517) 322–0030

Conservation and Tr.

Michigan Trail Rider.
1650 Ormond Road
White Lake, MI 48383-2
(810) 889–3624

Pigeon River Country Association
P.O. Box 122
Gaylord, MI 49735

Presque Isle Soil Conservation District
240 West Erie Street
Rogers City, MI 49779
(989) 734–4000

Rails-to-Trails Program
c/o Jim Radabaugh
Acting State Trails Coordinator
Forest Management Division
Michigan Department of Natural
    Resources
P.O. Box 30452
Lansing, MI 48909-7952
(517) 373–0367
E-mail: hagane@state.mi.us

Maps

Department of Natural Resources
    (DNR)
Information Services Center
Box 30028
Lansing, MI 48909

About the Author

Mike Modrzynski, an award-winning outdoor writer and photographer and active member of the Outdoor Writers Association of American, has left footprints in more than half of the fifty states but admits that he spends much more time fishing than hiking. A twenty-year career in the U.S. Air Force enabled him to travel extensively and, ultimately, return to his hometown of Rogers City, located on the Lake Huron shoreline in northeast lower Michigan.

Mike has written more than a thousand feature magazine articles in national and international publications, authored two other books—*Michigan Steelheading* and *Great Lake Steelhead Guide*—and contributed to two others. Love of the outdoors was instilled in him by his dad and nurtured over the years by the quiet corner of Michigan he grew up in.